はじめに

　一般財団法人国際コミュニケーション協会が出すデータをみると、TOEIC® L&R TEST は 2015 年に過去最高の年間 277 万人の受験者数にのぼり、過去 5 年でも年間 240 万人が平均して受験しています。そして、依然として単位認定や大学院入学試験、入社試験・会社の昇進の要件として扱われています。

　この状況から、英語の得手不得手や受験経験の有無にかかわらず、学生の時に単位のため、あるいは進学や就職のために TOEIC® L&R TEST を受ける可能性が非常に高いことが容易に想像できます。そこで、本書は、BASIC TEXTBOOK FOR THE TOEIC® L&R TEST（TOEIC® L&R TEST のための基礎演習）というタイトルの通り、TOEIC® L&R TEST の未受験者あるいはスコアが 300 点前後で伸びない初学習者が、半年から通年かけて英語の基礎力を培いながら TOEIC® L&R TEST で 550 点前後のスコアを目指せるような内容に作成されました。

　様々なレベルの学習者を、様々な教育現場で教えてきた TOEIC® L&R TEST に精通した経験豊富な執筆陣が、本書の随所で、単にスコアを上げるテクニックを提示するだけでなく、英語の基礎力や勉強方法を身に着け、結果的に TOEIC® L&R TEST のスコアも伸ばせるような工夫を凝らしています。具体的には、以下の 5 点を意識した構成になっています。

❶ 英文の基本的なルール・構造が理解できるような文法項目順に構成
❷ 英文中の単語・語句は TOEIC® L&R TEST 頻出のものに限定
❸ 短い英文のリピーティングやディクテイションの演習で音のルールを知り、リスニング力をアップ
❹ 本番レベルの模擬問題で応用力の確認
❺ 精読や英作文のコーナーを設け、丁寧な読解、ならびに表現を実際に使えるかをチェック

　本書を最大限に活用して、TOEIC® L&R TEST のスコアアップはもちろん、本当の意味で使える英語の素地を築いてください。本書を使い、一人でも多くの方が目標を達成されることを願っております。

編著者

【本書の略号・記号について】

文法解説で使用される記号

S：主語　　　　　　　O：目的語　　　　　C：補語
V：動詞の原形・原形不定詞・-(e)s を含む通常形
　Vp.：動詞の過去形　　　Vp.p.：動詞の過去分詞
　to V：to 不定詞　　　　Ving：動名詞／動詞の現在分詞

Words & Phrases で使用される記号

動：動詞　　　　名：名詞　　　　形：形容詞　　　　前：前置詞
副：副詞　　　　フ：フレーズ・定型表現

＊単語語尾の下線：品詞を特定するのに参考となる語尾に下線を付しています（p.14, Rule 6 参照）。

TOEIC® L&R TEST について

▶ TOEIC® とは

　TOEIC® とは、Test of English for International Communication の略で、英語によるコミュニケーション能力を測定する世界共通のテストです。TOEIC® テストは、ETS（Educational Testing Service）というアメリカのプリンストンにある非営利テスト開発機関によって開発・制作が行われています。現在、世界で約 150 か国、年間約 700 万人が受験し、日本でも大学の単位認定や、企業における人員採用および昇進要件、そして近年、大学の入学試験の一部としても利用されています。

▶ TOEIC® LISTENING & READING TEST の構成とスコア

　本書で扱う TOEIC® Listening & Reading Test（略称 TOEIC® L&R TEST）は、英語のリスニング（聴く力）とリーディング（読む力）を測定するテストです。解答方法は全てマークシート方式で、休憩なしの 120 分で 200 問が出題されます。テストは、設問も含め全て英語で構成されています。

リスニング・セクション（45 分：100 問）		リーディング・セクション（75 分：100 問）	
Part1： 写真描写問題	6 問	Part5： 短文穴埋め問題	30 問
Part2： 短文応答問題	25 問	Part6： 長文穴埋め問題	16 問
Part3： 会話問題	39 問	Part7： （1 つの文書）	29 問
Part4： 説明文問題	30 問	（複数の文書）	25 問

　スコアはリスニングとリーディングがそれぞれ 5～495 点の合計 10～990 点です。公開試験の場合、受験後 30 日以内に、団体特別制度（IP 試験）の場合、10 日以内にスコアが送付されます。

▶受験申込み方法

　公開試験は、インターネット（PC・携帯・スマートフォン）またはコンビニ端末で申込みが可能です。詳細は下記（財）国際ビジネスコミュニケーション協会のホームページをご参照ください。

▶ TOEIC® S/W（Speaking/Writing）

　本書では扱いませんが、TOEIC S/W という試験も行われています。これは、Speaking（話す）と Writing（書く）の力を測定する試験です。Speaking 20 分、Writing 60 分のテストで、各 200 点満点です。

TOEIC® L&R TEST 問い合わせ先：（一財）国際ビジネスコミュニケーション協会

〒 100-0014　東京都千代田区永田町 2-14-2　山王グランドビル

TEL：03-5521-6033　FAX：03-3581-4783（土・日・祝日・年末年始を除く 10:00～17:00）

https://www.iibc-global.org/toeic.html

BASIC TEXTBOOK FOR THE TOEIC® L&R TEST

TOEIC® L&R TEST の ための基礎演習

Tomohiro TSUCHIYA / Tatsuya NAKATA
Yuya NAKAGAWA / Noriko NAKANISHI
Yasunori NISHINA

SANSHUSHA

音声ダウンロード＆ストリーミングサービス（無料）のご案内

https://www.sanshusha.co.jp/onsei/isbn/9784384334975/

本書の音声データは、上記アドレスよりダウンロードおよびストリーミング再生ができます。ぜひご利用ください。

Download

Streaming

Contents

Unit 1 動詞

基本問題

① 1 文中の動詞の数は？

James ------- his job when he got a serious illness.

    (A) is quits   (B) to quit

    (C) quitting   (D) quit

② 主語と動詞の数(すう)の一致とは？

The kitchen at Southern General Hospital ------- enough meals for a small town.

    (A) to provide   (B) provide

    (C) provides   (D) providing

③ 動詞が原形で用いられる場面とは？

The size of the grant will usually ------- the work you have done.

    (A) depend on   (B) depends on

    (C) to be depended   (D) depending on

Unit 1 で押さえる文法のルール

Rule 1 英文 ＝ 1 つ以上の動詞が必要

Rule 2 1 文中の動詞の数 － 1 ＝ 1 文中の接続詞（等接以外）および関係詞の数

    ＊等接（等位接続詞）は and, but など、前後で同じ形（品詞）を結びつける接続詞

Rule 3 動詞の形は主語の数（単数か複数）に一致

Rule 4 動詞の原形を常に用いる場合

    ⇒　①命令文（Please ～等、文の冒頭に置く）

        ②助動詞がある（can, will, may の後ろに置く）

        ③不定詞表現がある（to [in order to / so as to] の後ろに置く）

　上記のルールを確認しながら、演習問題に取り組んでみましょう。必ず、どのルールが問われているのかを確認しながら問題にあたるようにしましょう。分からない語句にはチェックをし、問題を解き終わったら調べて、全体の文意を確認しましょう。

PART 5 (短文穴埋め問題)の演習

ポイント □ルールを意識しながら問題を解く　□分からない語句にチェック　□文意の確認

1. George's retirement ------- Molly to rethink her situation.
   - (A) lead
   - (B) to lead
   - (C) leading
   - (D) led

2. The successful applicant must ------- the main aim of his own project clearly.
   - (A) explains
   - (B) to explain
   - (C) explaining
   - (D) explain

3. When she arrives at the airport, she will immediately -------.
   - (A) check in
   - (B) checking in
   - (C) checks in
   - (D) be check in

4. The power plant in the northwestern province ------- electricity for most of the main island.
   - (A) provide
   - (B) to provide
   - (C) provides
   - (D) are providing

5. A number of research teams ------- responsible for the telephone surveys.
   - (A) to be
   - (B) are
   - (C) is
   - (D) being

6. For specific investments, please ------- your financial advisor.
   - (A) consulted
   - (B) consult
   - (C) consulting
   - (D) consults

7. The major instrument of central control over local activity ------- financial, because local authorities depend on central government.
   - (A) is
   - (B) to be
   - (C) have been
   - (D) are

8. Women's unemployment has risen at a faster rate than men's, although the actual number for men ------- much higher.
   - (A) remains
   - (B) remaining
   - (C) to remain
   - (D) remain

9. His method does not always ------- a unique result.
   - (A) to yield
   - (B) yielding
   - (C) yields
   - (D) yield

10. High-bandwidth cable could be helpful in order for people to ------- financial transactions online.
    - (A) conducting
    - (B) conduct
    - (C) being conducting
    - (D) conducts

PART 1 （写真描写問題）の演習 🎧01 ～ 🎧02

1.

Ⓐ　Ⓑ　Ⓒ　Ⓓ

2.

Ⓐ　Ⓑ　Ⓒ　Ⓓ

PART 2 （応答問題）の演習 🎧03 ～ 🎧05

3. Mark your answer on your answer sheet.　　Ⓐ　Ⓑ　Ⓒ

4. Mark your answer on your answer sheet.　　Ⓐ　Ⓑ　Ⓒ

5. Mark your answer on your answer sheet.　　Ⓐ　Ⓑ　Ⓒ

ディクテイションにチャレンジ！

Part 1 🎧01 ～ 🎧02

1. A: _____ the bike.

    B: _____ the building.

    C: The bike shop _____ the _____.

    D: The bike _____ into the wall.

2. A: _____ in his hand.

    B: The man is _____ the keyboard.

    C: The man is _____ an envelope.

    D: The man is _____ the letter.

Part 2 🎧03 ～ 🎧05

3. _____ do you _____?

    A: Almost _____.

    B: I like _____.

    C: You are a good _____.

4. _____ the software _____?

    A: I'm _____. _____.

    B: _____ model.

    C: Yes, _____.

5. _____?

    A: He _____.

    B: He _____.

    C: He _____.

9

PART 6（長文穴埋め問題）の演習

Questions 1-4 refer to the following advertisement.

Escape your .... city life and slow down to relax surrounded by the wonders of
1.
nature. Visit Acadia National Park and enjoy the beautiful Maine wilderness. Come to

take a rigorous hike to Thunder Hole, a rock structure in the ocean that .... an
2.
eruption of water every hour. Or, if you prefer less exciting activity, come in the fall

and walk the various footpaths while admiring the colorful fall leaves. .... For
3.
overnight accommodation, you can stay in a family-run bed and breakfast or choose

to camp in a tent under the stars. For more .... about Acadia National Park and
4.
overnight options, visit www.exploremaine.com/acadia.

1. (A) happy
   (B) busy
   (C) boring
   (D) angry

2. (A) causing
   (B) causes
   (C) to cause
   (D) cause

3. (A) Visit for the day or stay for the weekend.
   (B) The park is closed from October to March.
   (C) In the summer, call ahead to make restaurant reservations.
   (D) Thunder Hole erupts twice an hour in May and June.

4. (A) advertisements
   (B) information
   (C) opinions
   (D) travel places

精読コーナー❶

以下の英文を和訳してみましょう。PART 6, *line* 3

Come to take a rigorous hike to Thunder Hole, a rock structure in the ocean that causes an eruption of water every hour.

_____

_____

ポイント：1文中の動詞の数と関係詞の関係、中心［主節］の動詞の認識

➡ 文中にある動詞と関係詞を指摘しましょう。

Notes: □ rigorous 過酷な　□ eruption 噴出　□ footpath 小道

PART 7（読解問題）の演習

Questions 1-2 refer to the following announcement.

Randall To Talk On New Work *Hamlet and Its Mystery*

Adrian Randall, professor of English literature at the University of Toronto, will appear at the National Exhibition Center on November 4 from 6 p.m. to 8 p.m. Professor Randall will give a presentation on his new book, *Hamlet and Its Mystery*. After the presentation, he will sign copies of his book, which will be available for purchase at the center. This is a special not-to-be missed event.

1. What is the purpose of the announcement?
   (A) to introduce the University of Toronto
   (B) to promote books
   (C) to notify visitors of an event
   (D) to give a present to a speaker

2. Who is Adrian Randall?
   (A) He is the president of a university.
   (B) He specializes in literature.
   (C) He worked in the National Exhibition Center.
   (D) He is a presenter on a TV show.

精読コーナー❷

以下の英文を和訳してみましょう。PART 7, *line* 1

Adrian Randall, professor of English literature at the University of Toronto, will appear at the National Exhibition Center on November 4 from 6 p.m. to 8 p.m.

_____

_____

_____

ポイント：動詞と主語の特定、挿入部の扱い ➡ 動詞と主語を指摘しましょう!!

Notes: □ *Hamlet and Its Mystery*『ハムレットとその謎』(本の名前)
□ not-to-be missed 逃すべきでない

11

Unit 1　頻出 Words & Phrases

	W&P	発音	意味	Tips
☐1	**remain**	/riméɪn/	動 ～のままである	
☐2	**quit**	/kwɪt/	動 ～を辞める	
☐3	**grant**	/grænt|grɑːnt/	名 助成金	
☐4	**surround**	/səráund/	動 ～を囲む	be surrounded with/by 囲まれている
☐5	**rigorous**	/ríg(ə)rəs/	形 厳密な；厳格な	
☐6	**available**	/əvéɪləbl/	形 利用・入手できる	名 availability（→Unit 10）
☐7	**footpath**	/fútpæθ/	名 小道・歩道	＝trail 小道 / sidewalk 歩道
☐8	**provide**	/prəváɪd/	動 ～に提供する	provide A with B / provide B for [to] A A に B を提供する
☐9	**appear**	/əpíər/	動 登場する	名 appearance 登場；容姿
☐10	**copy**	/ká(:)pi /	名 1部；1冊	動 コピーする
☐11	**purchase**	/pə́:rtʃəs/	名 動 購入（する）	
☐12	**notify**	/nóutəfàɪ/	動 人に知らせる	㋬ notify 人 of … 人に…を知らせる
☐13	**envelope**	/énvəlòup/	名 封筒	
☐14	**latest**	/léɪtɪst/	形 最新の	＝state-of-the-art / up-to-date
☐15	**retirement**	/rɪtáɪərmənt/	名 退職	動 retire 退職する
☐16	**successful**	/səksésf(ə)l/	形 成功した	動 succeed 成功する 名 success 成功 形 successive 引き続いての
☐17	**applicant**	/ǽplɪk(ə)nt/	名 応募者	★語尾注意 動 apply 応募する（＋for）；当てはまる（＋to）
☐18	**immediately**	/ɪmíːdiətli/	副 すぐに	
☐19	**fold**	/fould/	動 ～を折る	形 folding 折りたたみの
☐20	**check in**		㋬ 手続する	⇔ check out（手続をして）出る
☐21	**financial**	/fənǽnʃ(ə)l, faɪ-/	形 金融の；財政の	副 financially 経済的な
☐22	**depend on**		㋬ ～に頼る	＝rely on
☐23	**yield**	/jiːld/	動 ～を生みだす	
☐24	**local**	/lóuk(ə)l/	形 地元の	副 locally 地元で；近所で
☐25	**method**	/méθəd/	名 方法	
☐26	**unique**	/ju(:)níːk/	形 独特な	
☐27	**helpful**	/hélpf(ə)l/	形 役に立つ	＝useful
☐28	**specialize in**		㋬ ～を専攻する	＝［米］major in
☐29	**get on**		㋬ ～に乗る	⇔get off
☐30	**responsible**	/rɪspá(:)nsəb(ə)l/	形 責任のある	㋬ be responsible for～ ～の責任がある

Unit 2 品詞と文型

基本問題

① 品詞とそのルールとは？

The ------- at the office are required to update their own computers every 6 months.

(A) employment   (B) in employing

(C) employ   (D) employees

---

② 品詞の並び順のルールと接辞による品詞の特定とは？

This teaching package has proved to be a very ------- product.

(A) popularize   (B) popular

(C) popularly   (D) popularity

---

③ 自動詞・他動詞、そして文型とは？

The survey ------- the firm to provide the most appropriate service overall.

(A) becomes   (B) imposes

(C) objects   (D) enables

Unit 2 で押さえる文法のルール

Rule 5 品詞の役割とルール

①名詞は文の主語・目的語・補語、形容詞は文の補語または名詞の修飾（下記③）として機能

名	動	名	名／形
主語(S)	動詞(V)	目的語(O)	補語 (C)

②前置詞（in, at, of など）は必ず名詞を従え、直前の名詞の修飾（形容詞の役割）か副詞の役割

< 前 … ＋ 名 >

＊…には③の各［パターン］の品詞が置かれる可能性があります

③名詞を直接修飾できるのは、形容詞か決定詞（a, an, the, some, no, any, his, their など）

［基本パターン］ 決 ＋ 名   ＊（可算）名詞が単数の場合は、決定詞が必要

形 ＋ 名

［応用パターン］ 決 ＋ 形 ＋ 名   ＊決定詞と形容詞がある場合の順番に注意

［頻出パターン］ 決 ＋ 副 ＋ 形 ＋ 名

Rule 6 頻出接辞と品詞の関係

【動詞の語尾】-fy, -ze, en-/-en, *ate* など
【形容詞の語尾】-al, -ic, -ful, -a/ible, *ate*, -ive, -a/ent, -ory, *-ed* など
【名詞の語尾】-ment, -s/tion, -e/ity, -ness, -a/ence, -ship,（動詞・名詞）＋ -e/or など
【副詞の語尾】（形容詞）＋ -ly, *-ed*

＊イタリックは他品詞の可能性があることを示します

Rule 7 文のパターンと大枠の意味

頻出パターン		大枠の意味	頻出動詞
SV	自動詞	S が V する、S がいる・ある	respond, apply, stay など
SVC		S＝C のようだ・ままだ、S ⇒ C になる	remain, seem, turn など
SVO	他動詞	S が O に [影響を与え] する	discuss, mention など
SVO to ~		S が O を~へ与える、あてる	assign, distribute など
SV 人 (to)* V'		S が人に V' する（依頼・援助・命令する / 可能にさせる）	ask, want, tell, help*, enable など
SVO$_1$O$_2$		S が O$_1$[人] に O$_2$[何か] を与える	give, send, offer など
SVOC V: 使役・知覚		[使役] S が O に C させるなど	make, let, get, keep など
		[知覚] S は O が C しているのを聞くなど	find, watch, hear など

＊ help の場合は、help 人 to V か help 人 V の 2 つのパターンがあります

PART 5 (短文穴埋め問題)の演習

ポイント □ルールを意識しながら問題を解く　□分からない語句にチェック　□文意の確認

1. ------- of the computer program is on schedule for late June.
   - (A) Ships
   - (B) In shipping
   - (C) Shipment
   - (D) Shipped

2. Only 9% of farmers and 12% of agricultural workers have agricultural -------.
   - (A) qualified
   - (B) qualifications
   - (C) qualify
   - (D) qualitative

3. For more information, please visit ------- new Web site.
   - (A) ours
   - (B) us
   - (C) our
   - (D) we

4. Managers can ------- ask for money back.
   - (A) easy
   - (B) easiness
   - (C) easily
   - (D) ease

5. The memorandum asked employees ------- a donation to the charity.
   - (A) makes
   - (B) made
   - (C) to make
   - (D) making

6. The office worker at the hospital ------- the family a copy of the pathologist's report.
   - (A) sent
   - (B) seemed
   - (C) submitted
   - (D) informed

7. Working groups for the creation of teaching materials can ------- educational activities more efficient.
   - (A) make
   - (B) take
   - (C) lead
   - (D) give

8. The economist remained ------- about the future of Asian economies.
   - (A) confidently
   - (B) confidence
   - (C) confident
   - (D) confidentiality

9. Suppliers may ------- a trade discount to customers in the same business.
   - (A) appear
   - (B) ask
   - (C) seem
   - (D) offer

10. The merger is taking a ------- longer time to finalize than expected.
    - (A) considerably
    - (B) considerable
    - (C) consider
    - (D) considerate

Notes: □ pathologist 病理学者

PART 2 （応答問題）の演習　 07 ～ 09

1. Mark your answer on your answer sheet.　　Ⓐ　Ⓑ　Ⓒ

2. Mark your answer on your answer sheet.　　Ⓐ　Ⓑ　Ⓒ

3. Mark your answer on your answer sheet.　　Ⓐ　Ⓑ　Ⓒ

PART 3 （会話問題）の演習　10

4. What does the man do?
   (A) He is a teacher.
   (B) He is a student.
   (C) He works at home.
   (D) He works at the student center.

5. What does the woman suggest the man do?
   (A) Try hard to find a job.
   (B) Submit his assignment next week.
   (C) Wait until next Friday.
   (D) Enroll in the course again.

ディクテイションにチャレンジ！

Part 2 🎧07 ~ 🎧09

1. _____ the new product?
    A: The _____ is.
    B: All the people are _____.
    C: He gave me a _____.

2. _____?
    A: No, the _____ the table.
    B: Yes, _____, please.
    C: _____, right?

3. _____?
    A: Yes, _____.
    B: _____ ?
    C: Actually _____.

シャドウイング＆オーバーラッピングからのペアワークにチャレンジ！

Part 3 🎧10

★「連結」「脱落」「同化」など音声変化に気を付けながら、音声を聞き、まずは後について発音してみましょう。次に、音声と同じスピードで発音してみましょう。発音と一緒に意味もとりながら挑戦してみましょう。以下、「連結」は _ の記号、「脱落」は ( ) で囲まれた箇所、「同化」は ▇ で表示しています。（131 ページ参照）

Woman: Dave, your assignmen(t) was due las(t) Friday. I'm afraid_I can'(t) le(t) you
        pass this course.

Man: Oh, I'm sorry, Ms. Brown. I have been busy with job hunting. Could you
        wait_until nex(t) week, please?

Woman: Well, it's the thir(d) time you didn'(t) submit your homework. Why don'(t)
        you try again_in the nex(t) semester?

Man: All right. Then_I'll go to the studen(t) center to sign_u(p) for the course
        again.

PART 6 （長文穴埋め問題) の演習

Questions 1-4 refer to the following article.

Pools company Littlewood, which has invested millions of pounds in new high-speed scanning equipment to check coupons, ------- ready to give other business organiza-
1.
tions the chance to use the equipment. Potential customers ------- the government,
2.
financial institutions, and market research organizations. A spokesperson for Littlewood said that the service was aimed toward users with a need to process huge numbers of documents. -------. The London-based operation has recently
3.
designed, developed and installed 25 new document scanning machines, each of which can handle up to 25,000 ------- an hour.
4.

1. (A) is
   (B) have been
   (C) to be
   (D) being

2. (A) inclusive
   (B) including
   (C) inclusion
   (D) include

3. (A) All documents are highly confidential.
   (B) The service would be only for financial business.
   (C) The new business would provide a more suitable use of the equipment.
   (D) New machines will be manufactured soon.

4. (A) conference calls
   (B) pools coupons
   (C) services
   (D) power cuts

Notes: □ confidential 秘密の　□ power cuts （outages/failure）停電

PART 7 (読解問題) の演習

Questions 1-3 refer to the following message.

FAX

FROM: Michael Gordon, ABC Legal Agency
FAX) 123-555-7891 / **TEL)** 123-555-7892
TO: MIT Furniture
ATTENTION: Mr. Smith, Orders Director
DATE: May/01/2013
RE: Shipment Order

This is to request that you send us the following items ASAP.

Item No. / Item	Quantity	Unit Price	Total
112---round table (brown)	1	$200.00	$200.00
201---sofa (black leather)	2	$175.00	$350.00
202---sofa (white leather)	3	$175.00	$525.00
301---curtain (beige)	4	$25.00	$100.00
			Total $1,175.00

If some of the items above are not in stock, we would be glad if you could dispatch products of similar color and shape. We would also be grateful if you would ship all the items together, not one by one.

Please send the items to the following address:
ABC Legal Agency
22 West River Street
Lancaster, LA 12345

Thank you for your attention.

1. To whom is this fax message being sent?
(A) The orders director at MIT Furniture
(B) Michael Gordon
(C) Mr. Smith at ABC Legal Agency
(D) The orders director at ABC Legal Agency

2. What would MIT Furniture be?
(A) A legal agency
(B) An advertisement agency
(C) A manufacture of home furniture
(D) A retailer of interior goods

3. What is the total charge for the sofas ordered?
(A) $450.00
(B) $625.00
(C) $875.00
(D) $975.00

1) 以下の英文を和訳してみましょう。PART 6, *line* 1

Littlewood, which has invested millions of pounds in new high-speed scanning equipment, is ready to give other business organizations the chance to use the equipment.

___

ポイント：中心 [主節] の動詞の認識と挿入句の読み方

➡ 挿入部分を指摘し、中心の動詞とその主語を指摘しなさい。

___

2) (   ) 内の語句を文法的に正しくなるよう並び替え全文を書き、和訳しなさい。PART 6, *line* 1

Littlewood (ready / is / to) give (chance / other business organization / to / the) use the equipment.

___

ポイント：品詞と品詞の並べ方、動詞の従える型

Unit 2　頻出 Words & Phrases 🎧11

	W&P	発音	意味	Tips
☐1	**introduce**	/ìntrədjúːs/	動 ～を紹介する	名 introduction 紹介
☐2	**due**	/djuː, duː/	形 締め切りのきた	句 due to（→Unit 4）
☐3	**submit**	/səbmít/	動 ～を提出する	＝句 hand in
☐4	**sign up for**		句 ～に登録する	＝動 register（→Unit 4）
☐5	**enroll in**		動 登録する	名 enrollment 入学；登録
☐6	**install**	/ɪnstɔ́ːl/	動 ～を設置する	名 installation 取り付け
☐7	**recently**	/ríːs(ə)ntli/	副 最近	形 recent 最近の
☐8	**potential**	/pəténʃ(ə)l/	形 見込みのある	
☐9	**invest**	/ɪnvést/	動 投資する (+ in)	
☐10	**-based**	/beɪst/	形 本社のある	
☐11	**process**	/prá(ː)ses/	動 ～を処理する 名 過程	
☐12	**design**	/dɪzáɪn/	動 ～を設計する	
☐13	**supplier**	/səpláɪər/	名 納品業者	≒ vendor
☐14	**customer**	/kʌ́stəmər/	名 (顧) 客	
☐15	**offer**	/ɔ́ːfər/	動 ～を提供する	句 offer O₁ O₂ / offer O₂ to O₁ O₁ に O₂ を提供する
☐16	**finalize**	/fáɪnəlàɪz/	動 ～を仕上げる	
☐17	**considerably**	/kənsíd(ə)rəbli/	副 かなり	形 considerable かなりの considerate 思いやりのある
☐18	**inform**	/ɪnfɔ́ːrm/	動 人に知らせる	句 inform 人 of …；人に ･･･ を知らせる＝notify（→Unit 1）
☐19	**present**	/prɪzént/	動 発表する	形 /préz(ə)nt/ 出席している；現在の
☐20	**efficient**	/ɪfíʃ(ə)nt/	形 効率の良い	
☐21	**confident**	/ká(ː)nfɪd(ə)nt/	形 自信がある	名 confidence 自信
☐22	**shipment**	/ʃípmənt/	名 配送	＝ shipping 動 ship ～を配送する
☐23	**employee**	/ɪmplɔ́ɪiː/	名 従業員	⇔employer 雇用主
☐24	**donation**	/dounéɪʃ(ə)n/	名 寄付 (金)	動 donate（→Unit 4）
☐25	**qualification**	/kwà(ː)lɪfɪkéɪʃ(ə)n/	名 資格 (証明書)	形 qualified 資格のある
☐26	**confidentiality**	/kà(ː)nfɪdenʃiǽləti/	名 内密；秘密性	
☐27	**merger**	/mə́ːrdʒər/	名 合併	動 merge (+with) ～と合併する
☐28	**assignment**	/əsáɪnmənt/	名 課題；任務	動 assign（→Unit 3）
☐29	**dispatch**	/dɪspǽtʃ/	動 ～を発送する	＝ ship
☐30	**attention**	/əténʃ(ə)n/	名 宛先；配慮；注意	句 Thank you for your attention. ご配慮いただきありがとうございます

Unit 3 受動態

基本問題

① 受動態の構造とは？

Several methods ------- at a staff meeting.

    (A) discuss

    (B) was discussed

    (C) discusses

    (D) were discussed

② 受動態の応用とは？

Normally, applicants will be ------- to an interview during the spring term.

    (A) continued

    (B) gone

    (C) invited

    (D) attended

③ 感情の動詞とその変化形の決定基準とは？

I am very ------- in the job you have advertised.

    (A) interesting

    (B) interest

    (C) interested

    (D) interests

Unit 3 で押さえる文法のルール

Rule 8　受動態の作り方と構造の特徴と例

能動態：　S　V　[O].　　　　　Tom broke　the vase.

受動態：　[O]　BE + Vp.p.　〈by S〉　The vase <u>was broken</u>　〈by Tom.〉

①目的語（O）をとる他動詞が受動態になる

②受動文は能動文から O が1つなくなる（O が S の位置に移動するため）

　⇔　他動詞で O がなければ受動態だと考える

＊動作が進行中の受動態：BE + *being* + Vp.p.（～が…されているところです。）

Rule 9 受動態の応用

① 受動態を作る一般動詞を選ぶ場合、受動態の主語（能動時の O）に注目
② 他動詞と同じ機能をする句動詞（自動詞＋前置詞）で、受動態が可能

【例】 Any suggestions will thoroughly **be *looked into*** by buyers.
  （どんな提案も仕入れ係によって徹底的に調べられます）

  ＊動詞 look は自動詞ですが、look into（〜を調べる）で一つの他動詞とみなします

Rule 10 「感情の動詞」の Vp.p. か Ving の選択基準

感情の動詞が置かれる位置	基準と変化形		
SVC の C	S が "人" ⇒ Vp.p.	S が "人以外" ⇒ Ving
SVOC の C	O が "人" ⇒ Vp.p.	O が "人以外" ⇒ Ving

【感情の動詞の例】

annoy　イライラさせる	surprise　驚かせる
satisfy　満足させる	frighten / scare　怖がらせる
interest　興味を持たせる	please / delight　喜ばせる
concern　心配させる	tire / exhaust　疲れさせる　など

ポイント □ルールを意識しながら問題を解く　□分からない語句にチェック　□文意の確認

1. A problem with a water pipe can easily ------- by a plumber.
   - (A) fix
   - (B) is fixed
   - (C) fixed
   - (D) be fixed

2. The California-based software company was ------- in 1988 by Richard.
   - (A) found
   - (B) finds
   - (C) founded
   - (D) founds

3. The first executive meeting has ------- because of schedule conflicts until next Monday.
   - (A) puts off
   - (B) been put off
   - (C) been putting off
   - (D) put off

4. This full-color guide ------- a comprehensive map of the Metro.
   - (A) contains
   - (B) is being contained
   - (C) containing
   - (D) was contained

5. I was very ------- with the accommodation arrangements.
   - (A) satisfy
   - (B) satisfying
   - (C) satisfies
   - (D) satisfied

6. We are also ------- strategies that will strengthen our position in the market, leading to a profitable expansion of our business in the future.
   - (A) implement
   - (B) implementing
   - (C) implementation
   - (D) implemented

7. The staff ------- to the project on a full-time or part-time basis.
   - (A) assigning
   - (B) is assigned
   - (C) being assigned
   - (D) assigned

8. The outcome of his business made him so -------.
   - (A) excites
   - (B) exciting
   - (C) excited
   - (D) excitement

9. The catalogue has been ------- to current customers and resellers.
   - (A) distributed
   - (B) submitted
   - (C) borrowed
   - (D) signaled

10. Men with a history of a heart problem ------- cholesterol lowering medicines.
    - (A) is given
    - (B) are gave
    - (C) give
    - (D) are given

リスニング・セクション

PART 1 （写真描写問題）の演習　🎧12 ～ 🎧13

1.

    Ⓐ　Ⓑ　Ⓒ　Ⓓ

2.

    Ⓐ　Ⓑ　Ⓒ　Ⓓ

PART 2 （応答問題）の演習　🎧14 ～ 🎧16

3. Mark your answer on your answer sheet.　　Ⓐ　Ⓑ　Ⓒ

4. Mark your answer on your answer sheet.　　Ⓐ　Ⓑ　Ⓒ

5. Mark your answer on your answer sheet.　　Ⓐ　Ⓑ　Ⓒ

Part 1 🎧12 ～ 🎧13

1. A: Some plates _____ from the counter.

    B: The cupboard _____.

    C: The woman _____ ladle.

    D: Dishcloths _____ on a rack.

2. A: The _____ by four women.

    B: The woman _____ men.

    C: The woman is _____ back.

    D: The _____ the woman's
       shoulders.

Part 2 🎧14 ～ 🎧16

3. _____ passengers were injured in the accident?

    A: _____ got hurt, _____ hospitalized.

    B: We _____ the news.

    C: The train _____ two hours.

4. Are _____ market?

    A: Yes, _____.

    B: Yes, _____.

    C: Yes, _____.

5. _____ the Tokyo office?

    A: _____.

    B: _____.

    C: Yes, I _____.

リーディング・セクション

PART 6（長文穴埋め問題）の演習

Questions 1-4 refer to the following letter.

April 10

Dear Ms. Houser,

Congratulations on being accepted to Pacific University! You are joining an incoming class of 246 students from 37 states and 18 countries. I am writing to ------- you to
1.
participate in our orientation program, Let's Get Started, from September 1 to 5. Each year, almost half of the incoming students attend orientation to make new friends, settle into their dormitories, and learn ------- the classes and extracurricular
2.
activities offered at Pacific University. If you are ------- in coming to Let's Get Started,
3.
please contact me at szehr@pacificuniversity.edu or 856-555-0413. -------. However,
4.
you must sign up before August 8.

Sincerely,

Sandy Zehr
Admissions Counselor
Pacific University

1. (A) beg
(B) suggest
(C) order
(D) invite

2. (A) from
(B) about
(C) with
(D) in

3. (A) interest
(B) interesting
(C) interests
(D) interested

4. (A) Only 75 students are eligible to participate.
(B) There is no limit to the number of participants.
(C) If you do not attend orientation, classes start September 9.
(D) Extracurricular activities start September 12.

Note: □ extracurricular activities 課外活動

Questions 1-3 refer to the following notice.

Dear Shareholders

You are cordially invited to attend the fourth British Gas Annual General Meeting, which will be held at the national Exhibition Centre on Thursday 9 August. The Meeting starts at 2:15 p.m. This gives the Board an opportunity to report to shareholders and to obtain their approval for resolutions that are voted upon at the Meeting. These resolutions cover the reappointment of Directors, the payment of dividends and the next annual meeting.

The following pages of this Notice of the Annual General Meeting give details of the business to be transacted at the Meeting. Some of the Notice may be complicated to understand. Therefore, we have added explanatory notes but if you have any queries, please telephone our Shareholder Enquiry Office, where the staff will be able to help you. The telephone number is 071-555-2000.

Yours sincerely,

Robert Evans
Chairperson and Chief Executive

1. What does the notice mainly inform shareholders of?
   (A) The British Gas Annual General Meeting
   (B) The reappointment of Directors
   (C) The explanatory notes
   (D) The telephone number of Shareholder Enquiry Office

2. What does the received approval for resolutions NOT cover?
   (A) The reappointment of Directors
   (B) The transaction of business
   (C) The payment of dividends
   (D) The next annual meeting

3. In the notice, the word "complicated" in paragraph 2, line 3, is closest in meaning to
   (A) comfortable
   (B) eligible
   (C) difficult
   (D) affordable

Notes: ☐ cordially 心から   ☐ dividend 配当金   ☐ explanatory note 注釈

精読コーナー

1) 以下の英文を和訳してみましょう。PART 7, *line* 1

You are cordially invited to attend the fourth British Gas Annual General Meeting, which will be held at the national Exhibition Centre on Thursday 9 August.

_____

_____

_____

ポイント：英文の構造を把握しよう

➡ 上記の英文から主語・動詞（受動態）部分を抜き出してみましょう。修飾部分（＜前置詞＋名詞＞や副詞）を除くのがこつ。

2) 指示代名詞（This）の指す内容を前ページの本文から明らかにして、和訳してみましょう。
PART 7, *line* 3

This gives the Board an opportunity to report to shareholders and to obtain their approval for resolutions that are voted upon at the Meeting.

_____

_____

ポイント：等位接続詞の扱い方

➡ 等位接続詞 and, but, or, nor などは、前後に等しい位（品詞・形）の語句を接続する役割を果たします。そして、時に列挙などを見つけるヒントにもなります。等位接続詞を見つけたら、

①等位接続詞の後ろの品詞・形を確認、

②等位接続詞の前で後ろと同じ形を探し、

③並列（A and/but/or B）関係

を確認しましょう。

◆上記の文で、等位接続詞 and が並列しているものを探してみましょう。

Unit 3 頻出 Words & Phrases

	W&P	発音	意味	Tips
☐1	**remove**	/rimúːv/	動 移す；取り除く	
☐2	**cupboard**	/kʌ́bərd/	名 食器棚	
☐3	**profitable**	/prá(ː)fətəb(ə)l/	形 利益のある	名 profit 利益（→Unit 12）
☐4	**delay**	/dɪléɪ/	動 遅らせる	= postpone / put off
☐5	**distribute**	/dɪstríbjuːt/	動 ～を配布する	= hand out ⇔ submit
☐6	**transfer**	/trǽnsfəːr/	動 転勤させる	
☐7	**beg**	/beg/	動 ～を懇願する	
☐8	**assign**	/əsáɪn/	動 ～を割り当てる	句 assign A to B A を B に割り当てる
☐9	**strategy**	/strǽtədʒi/	名 戦略	
☐10	**incoming**	/ínkʌ̀mɪŋ/	形 次に来る；後任の	
☐11	**attend**	/əténd/	動 ～に出席する	名 attendance 出席
☐12	**query**	/kwíəri/	名 質問	
☐13	**approval**	/əprúːv(ə)l/	名 承認	動 approve ～を承認する 形 approved 承認された
☐14	**arrangement**	/əréɪn(d)ʒmənt/	名 準備；計画	句 make arrangements for 準備する
☐15	**order**	/ɔ́ːrdər/	名 注文 動 ～を注文する	句 place an order 注文する
☐16	**dormitory**	/dɔ́ːrmətɔ̀ːri|-t(ə)ri/	名 寮；寄宿舎	
☐17	**dividend**	/dívɪdènd/	名 配当金	
☐18	**hang**	/hæŋ/	動 ～を（... に /... から）掛ける (+ on... / from...)	
☐19	**annual**	/ǽnju(ə)l/	形 年1回の	副 annually 毎年；年1度
☐20	**expansion**	/ɪkspǽnʃ(ə)n/	名 拡大	動 expand ～を拡大させる
☐21	**eligible**	/élɪdʒəb(ə)l/	形 資格のある	句 [be] eligible for... …の資格がある
☐22	**affordable**	/əfɔ́ːrdəbl/	形 手ごろな	= reasonable / inexpensive
☐23	**found**	/faʊnd/	動 ～を設立する	★活用注意 found-founded-founded
☐24	**executive**	/ɪgzékjətɪv/	名 形 幹部（の）	
☐25	**conflict**	/ká(ː)nflɪkt/	名 衝突	
☐26	**full-time**	/fùltáɪm/	形 正職員の	⇔ part-time パートの
☐27	**comprehensive**	/kà(ː)mprɪhénsɪv/	形 網羅的な	
☐28	**accommodation**	/əkà(ː)mədéɪʃ(ə)n/	名 宿泊施設	動 accommodate ～を収容する；応じる
☐29	**implement**	/ímplɪmènt/	動 ～を実行する	名 implementation 実施
☐30	**strengthen**	/stréŋθ(ə)n/	動 強固にする	形 strong 強い 名 strength 強さ

Unit 4 時制

基本問題

① 主節内の時制を決定する上で、大切なことは？

For a decade now, the company ------- a new model.

(A) will be producing   (B) is produced   (C) had produced   (D) has produced

② 「時制の一致」のルールとは？

They estimated that the cost in terms of benefits paid ------- to $8.

(A) will amount   (B) amounting   (C) amounted   (D) amount

③ 「時と条件を表す副詞節を導く接続詞とその節内の時制」のルールとは？

The President will abolish the informatics law when it ------- next year.

(A) will expire   (B) expires   (C) will have expired   (D) is expired

Unit 4 で押さえる文法のルール

Rule 11 主節の時制の決定方法

主節とは ⇒ 接続詞や関係詞を前に持たない動詞の節（SV...）

When the ceremony was over, Pearce left the venue last.

| | | S' | V' | | S | V |

接続詞   主　節

①文の時間	②動詞区分	③変化形決定	
過去 (-ed) *1	動作動詞 明確な終始を持つ数えられる行為：start, write, stay, travel など	進行形 (BE+Ving)	☑一時 / 同時性表現あり *2
☑過去表現あり		完了進行形 (HAVE+been+Ving)	☑短期間表現あり
未来 (will +)		完了形 (HAVE+Vp.p.)	☑期間 / 完結 / 回数表現あり
☑未来表現あり		普通形 (V)	☑上記以外 *3
現在	状態動詞 終始の曖昧な継続状態：have, know など	完了形 (HAVE+Vp.p.)	☑期間表現あり
上記以外		普通形 (V)	☑上記以外

注：*1 since + 過去時で「〜以来」という場合、主節の時間は現在時になることが多いので注意。
　　*2 「現在」＋「動作動詞」(往来発着・事前計画可能な動詞)＋「進行形」で、近い未来の事柄を表すことが可能。
　　*3 「現在」＋「動作動詞」＋「普通形」では、現在の習慣と反復の意味を表す。

Rule 12 「時制の一致」のルールとその例外

主節動詞の時間が過去になると、従属節内の時間も原則一致 !!　主節動詞が現在・未来の時間では、従属節の時間に制限はありません。

主節の時間	従属節が主節と同じ時間	従属節が主節より前の時間
過去	過去	大過去（had + Vp.p.）

【例外】 現在も変わらない状態・習慣　⇒　従属節中：現在

　　　　過去の事件（史実）　⇒　従属節中：過去

Rule 13 「時と条件を表す副詞節を導く頻出接続詞とその節内の時制」のルール

以下は、「時」と「条件」の副詞節を導く代表的な接続詞。

接続詞の区分	具体的な従属接続詞の例とその意味
時	when（～する時） once（一度～すると） as soon as（～するとすぐ）など
条件	if（～なら） unless（～でないなら）など

上記の接続詞がこの意味で利用される場合、未来の内容でも現在時にするので注意。

「時と条件を表す副詞節の中では未来のことも現在時で表す」というルールがあります。

PART 5 (短文穴埋め問題)の演習

ポイント □ルールを意識しながら問題を解く　□分からない語句にチェック　□文意の確認

1. TTE Ltd. ------- a product-launch event to announce new T-Phones tomorrow.
- (A) hold
- (B) will hold
- (C) holding
- (D) held

2. The bank ------- into the markets early yesterday to steady a bout of selling in the European markets.
- (A) steps
- (B) stepping
- (C) stepped
- (D) has stepped

3. She ------- journalism for 5 years when she moved to Britain in 2017.
- (A) studied
- (B) had been studying
- (C) has been studied
- (D) has studied

4. I thought that job applications ------- meant to be treated in confidence.
- (A) have been
- (B) is
- (C) would been
- (D) were

5. Once you ------- for the program, you will be invited to its events for free.
- (A) register
- (B) will register
- (C) registration
- (D) had registered

6. Wage negotiations between labor and management ------- for almost 2 years.
- (A) takes place
- (B) have been taking place
- (C) had been taken place
- (D) has taken place

7. When I got back, Pat asked me if I ------- a good holiday.
- (A) had had
- (B) have been had
- (C) had
- (D) have

8. She was a housekeeper who ------- by the family for 23 years.
- (A) has been employing
- (B) had employed
- (C) to be employed
- (D) had been employed

9. In order to check stock prices, my father ------- the 7 o'clock news every evening.
- (A) has been watched
- (B) watches
- (C) watching
- (D) has watching

10. One official admits that the program will fail unless the transport problem -------.
- (A) solves
- (B) will be solved
- (C) is solved
- (D) will have solved

PART 2 （応答問題）の演習　18 ～ 20

1. Mark your answer on your answer sheet.　Ⓐ　Ⓑ　Ⓒ

2. Mark your answer on your answer sheet.　Ⓐ　Ⓑ　Ⓒ

3. Mark your answer on your answer sheet.　Ⓐ　Ⓑ　Ⓒ

PART 4 （説明文問題）の演習　21

4. Who most likely is the speaker?
   (A) A project leader.
   (B) A sales representative.
   (C) A company shareholder.
   (D) A marketing consultant.

5. How long has Nancy been working in the Sales Department?
   (A) For a year.
   (B) For 2 years.
   (C) For 3 years.
   (D) For 4 years.

6. What will the team members do tomorrow?
   (A) They will appoint the competent worker.
   (B) They will start working on the new project.
   (C) They will frighten Nancy.
   (D) They will start looking for a new job.

ディクテイションにチャレンジ！

Part 2 🎧18 ～ 🎧20

1. _____ attend the conference?

    A: Yes, _____.

    B: No, _____ another conference.

    C: Yes. _____ the contract.

2. Have you _____ version of this document?

    A: _____ tomorrow.

    B: _____. Have you?

    C: Yes. _____ this morning.

3. _____ the wooden crates to the warehouse?

    A: He _____.

    B: _____.

    C: _____ perfume.

シャドウイング＆オーバーラッピングにチャレンジ！

Part 4 🎧21

★「連結」「脱落」「同化」など音声変化に気を付けながら、音声を聞き、まずは後について発音してみましょう。次に、音声と同じスピードで発音してみましょう。発音と一緒に意味もとりながら挑戦してみましょう。

It_is_a grea(t) pleasure for me to welcome Nancy Smith to our R & D Department. Nancy has been working as one_of the most competen(t) representatives in the Sales Depar(t)ment for these last four years, an(d) will be joining us a(t) the launch of_our new projec(t) starting tomorrow. Nancy, we are more than thrill(ed) to have you here as_a member of_our team. We hope, sincerely, that you will find the new R & D project as interesting and_exciting as we all do. Here's wishing you a great new start, and here's wishing the team a bright future!

PART 6 (長文穴埋め問題) の演習

Questions 1-4 refer to the following notice.

Smart Supplier's Concert and Opening Sale

------. Tickets for the concert will be on sale at Old Town in San Diego. The
1.
concert is scheduled to be held on August 25th at 6:00 p.m. Proceeds from the

concert ------- to the Charity Society of San Diego.
2.

If you ------- more information about this concert, call us on 212-555-0055.
3.

Smart Supplier's Opening Sale will be held on August 26th from 8:00 am to 8:00

p.m. All products will have an additional 30% ------- on the 26th, 27th, and 28th.
4.

We also have a day care center for parents who wish to relax while shopping.

Thank you for your time and see you soon!

---

1. (A) Old Town will be reconstructed to attract visitors.
  (B) Smart Supplier will sponsor a local concert for the people of San Diego.
  (C) Opening sales this time will be up by 5 percent.
  (D) The concert tickets will be available only on the website.

2. (A) to donate
  (B) donating
  (C) will be donated
  (D) was donated

3. (A) will require
  (B) require
  (C) required
  (D) had required

4. (A) discount
  (B) disagreement
  (C) disappointment
  (D) disclosure

PART 7（読解問題）の演習

Questions 1-2 refer to the following text message chain.

Paula Stacey | 8:14 am

I wonder if I could be late for the sales meeting at 9 o'clock this morning. I'm on the train, but it has stopped due to a fault.

Robert Dobson | 8:20 am

Sorry to hear that. But aren't you making a presentation on a new sales project?

Paula Stacey | 8:22 am

Yes. And that makes me feel more nervous and irritated. Are you in the meeting room? Is Geoffrey there?

Robert Dobson | 8:23 am

Yes, he is. Is there anything I should tell him?

Paula Stacey | 8:25 am

Geoffrey, an accounting manager, is also involved in the new project and I guess he has the same material to be used for today's meeting. Could you ask him if he can present the project on my behalf?

Robert Dobson | 8:26 am

Certainly. CUL.

Paula Stacey | 8:26 am

Thanks for your help.

Note: □ CUL (= See you later の略)

1. What is NOT suggested about
   Ms. Stacey?
   (A) She is commuting by rail.
   (B) She is involved in a sales project.
   (C) Her working division is accounting.
   (D) She thanks Robert for his help.

2. What does Mr. Dobson mean when he
   writes, "Certainly"?
   (A) He is happy to help Ms. Stacey.
   (B) He is certain that Ms. Stacey will
       be on time.
   (C) He will give a gift to Geoffrey.
   (D) He is ready to account for the
       cancellation of today's presentation.

精読コーナー

以下の英文を時制に注意して和訳してみましょう。

❶ PART 6, *line* 5

The Opening Sale will be held on August 26th.

ポイント：時間と受動態

❷ PART 4, *line* 2

Nancy has been working as a sales person for these four years.

ポイント：期間と変化形

PART 5 応用

❸ Wilson Ltd. has maintained a continuous growth in sales since the company was founded in 1987.

ポイント：Sinceのある時制

PART 5 応用

❹ All boxes will have been removed from the workroom by noon.

ポイント：進行形と受動態

Unit 4 頻出 Words & Phrases 22

	W&P	発音	意味	Tips
☐ 1	**require**	/rikwáɪər/	動 ～を要求する	名 require<u>ment</u> 資格；必要品
☐ 2	**confer<u>ence</u>**	/ká(:)nf(ə)r(ə)ns/	名 会議	句 conference call 電話会議
☐ 3	**contract**	/ká(:)ntrækt/	名 契約	
☐ 4	**appoint**	/əpóɪnt/	動 ～を指名する	名 appoint<u>ment</u> 指名；予約（→Unit10）
☐ 5	**sales**	/seɪlz/	名 売上高	句 on sale（特売）販売で
☐ 6	**representa<u>tive</u>**	/rèprɪzéntətɪv/	名 形 代表（の）	★語尾注意
☐ 7	**launch**	/lɔːn(t)ʃ/	名 動 開始（する）	
☐ 8	**addi<u>tional</u>**	/ədíʃ(ə)n(ə)l/	形 追加の	句 in addi<u>tion</u> (to)（～に）加えて
☐ 9	**due to**		句 ～が原因で	＝because of, on account of
☐ 10	**accounting**	/əkáuntɪŋ/	名 会計	句 accounting depart<u>ment</u> 経理課
☐ 11	**involv<u>ed</u>**	/ɪnvá(:)lvd/	形 関係して	句 [be] involved in... …に関わっている
☐ 12	**on one's behalf**		句 （人）の代わりに	＝in one's place
☐ 13	**account for**		句 ～を説明する；～を占める	～を占める
☐ 14	**announce**	/ənáuns/	動 ～を発表する	名 announce<u>ment</u> 公表
☐ 15	**journalism**	/dʒə́:rnəlìz(ə)m/	名 ジャーナリズム	
☐ 16	**register**	/rédʒɪstər/	動 ～を登録する	＝sign up for / enroll in
☐ 17	**cancella<u>tion</u>**	/kænsəléɪʃ(ə)n/	名 取り消し	動 cancel ～を取り消す；中止にする
☐ 18	**solve**	/sa(:)lv/	動 ～を解決する	名 solu<u>tion</u> 解決策
☐ 19	**unless**	/ənlés/	接 ～でないなら	
☐ 20	**negotia<u>tion</u>**	/nɪgòuʃiéɪʃ(ə)n/	名 交渉	動 negotia<u>te</u> 交渉する
☐ 21	**wage**	/weɪdʒ/	名 賃金	
☐ 22	**labor**	/léɪbər/	名 労働	
☐ 23	**manage<u>ment</u>**	/mǽnɪdʒmənt/	名 経営；管理	
☐ 24	**applica<u>tion</u>**	/æplɪkéɪʃ(ə)n/	名 申込み	句 application form 願書
☐ 25	**stock**	/sta(:)k/	名 株；在庫	句 in stock 在庫のある ⇔ out of stock 在庫切れの
☐ 26	**transport**	/trænspɔ:rt/ /trænspɔ́:rt/	名 交通；輸送 動 ～を輸送する	名 transporta<u>tion</u> 交通／輸送機関
☐ 27	**carry out**		句 ～を実行する	
☐ 28	**donate**	/dóuneɪt/	動 ～を寄付する	名 donation
☐ 29	**crate**	/kreɪt/	名 木箱	
☐ 30	**compe<u>tent</u>**	/ká(:)mpət(ə)nt/	形 有能な	

Unit 5 動名詞と不定詞

基本問題

① **目的語に動名詞を選ぶか to 不定詞を選ぶか？**

I have just finished ------- this booklet.

    (A) to read   (B) reading   (C) read   (D) being read

② **to 不定詞の副詞的用法の意味の決定方法は？**

We planned and performed an audit ------- all the information.

    (A) so as to obtain   (B) to be obtained

    (C) in order to obtained   (D) so as not to obtaining

③ **動名詞、to 不定詞を含むフレーズとは？**

In language teaching, teachers have become accustomed to ------- audiobooks.

    (A) use   (B) be used by   (C) using   (D) being used

Unit 5 で押さえる文法のルール

Rule 14 動名詞と to 不定詞のイメージと役割

	イメージ	役割		
		名詞	形容詞	副詞
動名詞	既存・進行中	○	×	×
to 不定詞	これから（未来）	○ *1	○	○ Rule 15

＊1：前置詞の目的語としては利用しない（× ＜前＋ to V［名詞］ ＞）

＊準動詞の主語が文の主語と一致しない場合、以下の形で意味上の主語を明示

  【動名詞】S'（所有格 / 目的格）Ving   【to 不定詞】for S（目的格）to V

Rule 15 to 不定詞の副詞的用法の 6 つの意味

意味	備考
目的	in order (not) to / so as (not) to V でも用いる
感情の原因	直前に感情を表す表現（S <be> happy / sad to V など）
判断の根拠	直前に判断を表す表現（It <be> natural / odd to V など）
条件	文頭が比較的多い To V〜,
程度	too 〜 to V / enough to V
結果	文末で、(only) to V など の形で

PART 5 (短文穴埋め問題)の演習

ポイント □ルールを意識しながら問題を解く　□分からない語句にチェック　□文意の確認

1. Making effective oral presentations in public ------- not the same as talking with friends in conversations.
   (A) have been
   (B) to be
   (C) are
   (D) is

2. For a long time, he has denied ------- meetings with A&S Ltd.
   (A) to hold
   (B) to be held
   (C) holding
   (D) hold

3. The firm agreed ------- emissions of pollutants by 50 percent by 2020.
   (A) to reduce
   (B) reducing
   (C) reduces
   (D) to be reduced

4. The bank will keep the company from bankruptcy by ------- a reorganization plan.
   (A) to accept
   (B) acceptance
   (C) accepting
   (D) being accepted

5. Mr. Orlando was ------- to step down despite his popularity with his coworkers.
   (A) considered
   (B) admitted
   (C) enjoyed
   (D) forced

6. Even in big companies, it is very hard for all employees ------- despondent.
   (A) to not feel
   (B) to be felt
   (C) not to feel
   (D) not feeling

7. Would you mind ------- this report to my supervisor?
   (A) to hand in
   (B) your handing in
   (C) hand in
   (D) my handing in

8. A new consultative group was set up ------- the new program.
   (A) to overseeing
   (B) overseeing
   (C) to oversee
   (D) to be overseen

9. This new treatment is worth ------- for other patients in a similar situation.
   (A) to consider
   (B) considers
   (C) considering
   (D) being considered

10. This booklet gives you guidance on ------- deal with the problem in workplace.
    (A) methods
    (B) how to
    (C) manner
    (D) in order to

PART 1 （写真描写問題）の演習　23 ～ 24

1.

Ⓐ　Ⓑ　Ⓒ　Ⓓ

2.

Ⓐ　Ⓑ　Ⓒ　Ⓓ

PART 2 （応答問題）の演習　25 ～ 27

3. Mark your answer on your answer sheet.　Ⓐ　Ⓑ　Ⓒ

4. Mark your answer on your answer sheet.　Ⓐ　Ⓑ　Ⓒ

5. Mark your answer on your answer sheet.　Ⓐ　Ⓑ　Ⓒ

ディクテイションにチャレンジ！

Part 1 🎧23 ～ 🎧24

1. A: Lampposts _____.
   B: Some chairs _____.
   C: A _____ on the patio.
   D: _____ soon.

2. A: People have _____ the ball.
   B: People have _____ the ball.
   C: People are _____ the ball.
   D: People are _____ the ball.

Part 2 🎧25 ～ 🎧27

3. _____ to the city hall?
   A: _____ the mayor.
   B: _____ the city hall.
   C: _____.

4. _____ jogging in the morning?
   A: I _____ in the evening.
   B: I _____ very much.
   C: I _____.

5. _____ a little louder? I can't hear you.
   A: _____.
   B: Sorry. _____ to the microphone.
   C: I _____ before.

PART 6 (長文穴埋め問題) の演習

Questions 1-4 refer to the following notice.

Dear Valued Member,

From May 5 to June 2, ABC Fit Health Club will be closed for remodeling. We are ------- old weight-lifting machines with new ones, as well as expanding our cardio area
1.
to accommodate the increased demand. During the construction, the club will not be open to members.

In order to ------- you a place to exercise, our friend Planet Health has agreed to
2.
accept our members during this period. If you go to Planet Health and show your ABC Fit Health Club membership card, you will be able to take advantage of their facilities free of charge. -------. All of their equipment and facilities are in good
3.
condition.

Thank you for your understanding and -------. We look forward to welcoming you back
4.
to ABC Fit Health Club on June 3.

Taylor Swartz
Manager

---

1. (A) buying
　(B) replacing
　(C) keeping
　(D) borrowing

2. (A) giving
　(B) be given
　(C) have been given
　(D) give

3. (A) Planet Health's membership fee will increase next month.
　(B) ABC Fit Health Club does not accept Planet Health members.
　(C) Planet Health offers cardio machines, free weights, locker rooms, and a lap pool.
　(D) We apologize for the inconvenience.

4. (A) patience
　(B) difficulty
　(C) feedback
　(D) time

Note: □ cardio 有酸素運動

PART 7 (読解問題)の演習

Questions 1-3 refer to the following program review.

September 9th — Editor's Picks on Channel 1
8:00 p.m. — The Rifles Remembered If you grew up listening to The Rifles singing energetic pop songs on the radio, this tribute to the wonderful music band will take you back in time. Includes rare video clips from their memorable concert at New York stadium in 1985. The band members' back stories will also be introduced.
9:00 p.m. — Mystery of Meteors This 60-minute program reveals the mystery of meteors falling to earth. Don't miss these incredible scenes of various meteors and their mysterious story. Commentary by Japanese astronaut Kenji Yamamoto.
10:30 p.m. — Human Evolution Revisited This is one of the best documentaries about a complete timeline of human evolution. This program shows the evolutionary process leading up to the appearance of modern humans including the emergence of Homo sapiens. Insightful comments are given by Prof. Susan Hyland at Lincoln University. You must see it!!

1. What are the three programs featured in the review mainly about?
(A) Weapons, falling stars, and evolution of human beings
(B) Music, mystery of the earth, and evolution of industry
(C) Music, falling stars, and evolution of human beings
(D) Weapons, mystery of the earth, and evolution of industry

2. Which show will Kenji Yamamoto appear in?
(A) The Rifles Remembered
(B) Mystery of Meteors
(C) Human Evolution Revisited
(D) None of the above

3. Which program will be aired from 10 p.m. on Channel 1?
(A) The Rifles Remembered
(B) Mystery of Meteors
(C) Human Evolution Revisited
(D) None of the above

Notes: ☐ tribute 記念

45

以下、各英文の下線部を適切な形に直して和訳しましょう。

❶ PART 5, (1)

Making oral presentations in public <u>be</u> not the same as talking with friends.

_____

ポイント：準動詞は単数か複数扱いどちらか

❷ PART 2, (3)

Would you mind <u>speak</u> a little louder?

_____

ポイント：動詞mindの意味とVing/toV

❸ PART 1, (1)

The runner is trying <u>tie</u> her shoelaces.

_____

ポイント：動詞tryの意味とVing/toV

❹ PART 6, _line_ 10

We look forward to <u>welcome</u> you back to Fit Health Club.

_____

ポイント：look forward toのtoの品詞

❺ PART 6, _line_ 5

In order to <u>be given</u> you a place to exercise, our friend Planet Health has agreed <u>accept</u> our members during this period.

_____

ポイント：giveの基本文型、agreeの意味とVing/toV

Unit 5　頻出 Words & Phrases 🎧28

		W&P	発音	意味	Tips
☐	1	**insightful**	/ínsàitf(ə)l/	形 洞察力に富んだ	名 insight 洞察（力）
☐	2	**audit**	/ɔ́:dət/	動 名 （〜の）会計監査（をする）	
☐	3	**demand**	/dɪmǽnd/	名 需要 動 〜を要求する	句 demand + that S (should) V V するよう要求する
☐	4	**agree**	/əgríː/	動 賛成する、同意する (+ with / to V)	名 agreement 同意；契約
☐	5	**booklet**	/búklət/	名 パンフレット	= brochure / pamphlet
☐	6	**take advantage of**		句 〜を利用する	
☐	7	**free of charge**		句 無料で	= (for) free / at no cost
☐	8	**worth**	/wə́:rθ/	形 価値がある	句 be worth Ving V する価値がある
☐	9	**patio**	/pǽtiòu/	名 中庭	
☐	10	**equipment**	/ɪkwípmənt/	名 装置；機器	動 equip 〜を備え付ける
☐	11	**accept**	/əksépt/	動 〜を受け入れる	名 acceptance 受諾
☐	12	**review**	/rivjú:/	名 批評	動 再検討する
☐	13	**feature**	/fí:tʃər/	動 〜を特集する	名 特徴
☐	14	**step down**		句 辞職する	
☐	15	**despite**	/dɪspáit/	前 〜に関わらず	= 句 in spite of
☐	16	**popularity**	/pà(:)pjəlǽrəti/	名 人気	形 popular 人気の 動 popularize 〜を一般に普及させる
☐	17	**coworker**	/kóuwə̀:rkər/	名 同僚	= colleague
☐	18	**oversee**	/òuvərsíː/	動 監督する	= supervise
☐	19	**hand in**		句 〜を提出する	= submit ⇔ hand out
☐	20	**supervisor**	/sú:pərvàizər/	名 監督；指導教授	⇔ subordinate 部下 （→Unit 6）
☐	21	**reduce**	/ridjú:s/	動 〜を減らす	名 reduction ⇔ increase
☐	22	**deny**	/dɪnái/	動 〜を否定する	句 deny Ving V することを否定する
☐	23	**consider**	/kənsídər/	動 〜をよく考える	句 condisder Ving V することを熟考する
☐	24	**deal with**		句 〜を処理する	= cope with / handle / treat 名 deal 取引；契約
☐	25	**memorable**	/mém(ə)rəb(ə)l/	形 記憶すべき；素晴らしい	
☐	26	**workplace**	/wə́:rkplèis/	名 職場	
☐	27	**admit**	/ədmít/	動 〜を認める	名 admission 入会；入場料
☐	28	**stack**	/stæk/	動 〜を積み重ねる	≒ pile 積み上げる
☐	29	**firm**	/fə:rm/	名 会社	
☐	30	**fee**	/fi:/	名 料金、手数料	句 license fee / management fee / admission fee 許可料／管理費／入場料

Unit 6 現在分詞と過去分詞

基本問題

① （形容詞的）分詞の形（Ving / Vp.p.）の決め方とは？

The building is a day-care center ------- by a volunteer organization.

    (A) operation

    (B) operating

    (C) operate

    (D) operated

② 副詞的分詞（いわゆる分詞構文）の形（Ving / Vp.p.）の決め方とは？

------- in a good residential area, this house is perfect for our family.

    (A) Locating

    (B) Location

    (C) Located

    (D) Locate

③ 使役動詞・知覚感覚動詞の目的語補語に置かれる分詞・不定詞の決定は？

Please let me ------- if you have any concerns with this plan.

    (A) to know

    (B) know

    (C) knowing

    (D) known

Unit 6 で押さえる文法のルール

Rule 16 分詞の形（Ving（現在分詞）か Vp.p.（過去分詞））を決定する基準

分詞の種類	基準	名詞 / 主語が～する	名詞 / 主語が～される
形容詞的分詞	修飾する名詞	Ving	Vp.p.
副詞的分詞 （分詞構文）	主節の主語	Ving	Vp.p.

Rule 17 副詞的分詞（分詞構文）の5つの用法

意味	時	理由	条件	譲歩	付帯状況
和訳	～の時	～して	～なら	～だが	～しながら

【副詞詞的分詞（分詞構文）の注意事項】

①どの意味が適切かは、主節との関係で判断。

②文頭の Being/Having been は省略されることが多いので注意。

③意味を強調するため、分詞の直前に接続詞を置くことがあります（主節の主語との一致が条件）。

Rule 18 SVOC 文型をとる頻出の動詞と C の位置にくる分詞の決定（Ving か Vp.p.）

SVOC をとる頻出動詞	動詞 — C に置かれる形
使役動詞	let — V
	make — V / Vp.p.
	have — V / Ving / Vp.p.
	get — to V / Ving / Vp.p.
知覚感覚動詞	see / hear / feel など — V / Ving / Vp.p ＊ to V は置かない
その他	keep / leave など — Ving / Vp.p.

注：V/Ving/Vp.p. の選択は O との関係（「O が V する / している / される」）で決定

ポイント □ルールを意識しながら問題を解く　□分からない語句にチェック　□文意の確認

1. If retailers buy in large quantities, the manufacturer will provide the goods at a slightly ------- price.
    (A) reduction
    (B) reduce
    (C) to reduce
    (D) reduced

2. Although the new scheme appears to be the manager's ------- option, his subordinates doubt whether it works.
    (A) preferred
    (B) preferring
    (C) preferably
    (D) prefer

3. Online orders ------- the credit limit are subject to additional fees or closure of the account.
    (A) excessive
    (B) exceed
    (C) exceeded
    (D) exceeding

4. Simply ------- with beautiful illustrations, the book containing the best-known fairy tales is very popular.
    (A) writing
    (B) written
    (C) to write
    (D) writes

5. I made my subordinates ------- about the future plan of their business.
    (A) talk
    (B) to talk
    (C) talking
    (D) talked

6. One of the ------- developments in biology over the past few years has been the identification of the specific genes to cause cancer.
    (A) excite
    (B) excited
    (C) exciting
    (D) to excite

7. ------- by Jack Straw in 1977, the firm started out as a computer bureau.
    (A) Found
    (B) To found
    (C) Founded
    (D) Founding

8. ------- my agency's research, music is becoming a sensitive issue among consumers.
    (A) Judged from
    (B) Judgment from
    (C) Judging from
    (D) Judge from

9. I saw Richard ------- the water tank on the premises.
    (A) inspected
    (B) inspecting
    (C) inspection
    (D) to inspect

10. ------- 20 years working with local planning authorities, he is going to start working at Bovis Homes as a town planner.
    (A) Spent
    (B) Having spent
    (C) Having been spent
    (D) To spend

リスニング・セクション

PART 2 (応答問題) の演習　🎧29 ～ 🎧31

1. Mark your answer on your answer sheet.　Ⓐ　Ⓑ　Ⓒ

2. Mark your answer on your answer sheet.　Ⓐ　Ⓑ　Ⓒ

3. Mark your answer on your answer sheet.　Ⓐ　Ⓑ　Ⓒ

PART 3 (会話問題) の演習　🎧32

4. What are the speakers mainly discussing?
   (A) New employees' training
   (B) A planned picnic
   (C) Registration for a seminar
   (D) A delivery deadline

5. What does the woman say about Susan?
   (A) She works at a cash register.
   (B) She works in the personnel department.
   (C) She works for a travel agency.
   (D) She works for the information service center.

6. What will the man do next?
   (A) He will hold the event.
   (B) He will sign up.
   (C) He will meet the picnic participants.
   (D) He will recruit an employee with interpersonal skills.

Part 2 🎧29 ～ 🎧31

1. _____ do with this PC? _____ right.

    A: _____.

    B: Computer science is _____.

    C: You _____.

2. _____ job hunting, right?

    A: Yes, _____ a publishing company.

    B: Yes, _____ Hong Kong before.

    C: Yes, I'll tell _____.

3. Can you recognize _____?

    A: _____ in this room.

    B: He was _____ of our department.

    C: _____.

シャドウイング＆オーバーラッピングからのペアワークにチャレンジ！

Part 3 🎧32

★「連結」「脱落」「同化」など音声変化に気を付けながら、音声を聞き、まずは後について発音してみましょう。次に、音声と同じスピードで発音してみましょう。発音と一緒に意味もとりながら挑戦してみましょう。

Woman A: Have you signed_up for the upcoming company picnic, Ted?

Man: Sorry, no. What_is tha(t)?

Woman A: Didn't you read yesterday's memorandum_or check_it_on the notice board? Mos(t) new employees will probably join the picnic.

Man: Really? Do you know when the dea(d)line for signing up_is?

Woman A: No, but Susan_in the personnel_office is_in charge o(f) the registration. Oh, wait. Hello, Susan, how are you doing? I was jus(t) talking about you. Tell me, are you still_accepting registrations for the next company picnic?

Woman B: Yes, I am. Any time by the end_o(f) this week, Friday 13th.

Woman A: Oh great! Ted really wants to go along.

Woman B: Many new recruits_are coming, so you shoul(d) join_in an(d) ge(t) to know people. You'll have_a grea(t) time.

Man: Thank you very much for letting me know. I'll register a(s) soon as_I can.

リーディング・セクション

PART 6 (長文穴埋め問題) の演習

Questions 1-4 refer to the following information.

Current Airways Luggage Policy

Before you arrive at N.Y. international airport, please visit the U.S. Transportation Security Administration website at www.tsa.gov for a current listing of all illegal items. All types of containers with fuel will -------.
  1.
-------, all other types of liquids may be prohibited in carry-on luggage.
  2.
Items ------- to be carried on board are limited to one piece of carry-on luggage plus
  3.
one personal item, such as a purse, small file case, briefcase, camera case, backpack, or laptop computer. Some airlines require a carry-on fee. -------.
  4.

---

1. (A) reject
   (B) have rejected
   (C) be rejected
   (D) are rejected

2. (A) In addition
   (B) On the whole
   (C) In contrast
   (D) Instead

3. (A) allow
   (B) allowing
   (C) allowed
   (D) allows

4. (A) In order to check flight status, visit our website.
   (B) Carry-on luggage to any airplanes is not permitted.
   (C) For more information, contact airline personnel.
   (D) Most of the airlines offer you a free boarding pass.

Questions 1-3 refer to the following letter.

Dear Mr Smith

Many thanks for your fax today. [1] We are happy to be able to confirm your reservation with us for one double room on the evening of July 6th. [2] This price is inclusive of all state and federal taxes, full buffet continental breakfast, all facilities and a morning newspaper. [3] We would like to thank you again for your patronage and look forward to welcoming you to our establishment. [4]

Sincerely yours,

Gloria Davis, Reservations Manager

1. What type of place is this establishment?
   (A) Garden
   (B) Museum
   (C) Airline company
   (D) Hotel

2. In which of the position marked [1], [2], [3], and [4] does the following sentence best belong?

   "A total of $120 will be charged as requested to your credit card."

   (A) [1]
   (B) [2]
   (C) [3]
   (D) [4]

3. What is NOT included in the price?
   (A) State taxes
   (B) Gym
   (C) A newspaper
   (D) Breakfast

Notes: ☐ identification 検証；識別　☐ gene 遺伝子

精読コーナー

1) 以下、中心の文の要素（動詞・主語・目的語など）を特定しながら、和訳しましょう。

PART 5, (3)

Orders exceeding the credit limit will be subject to additional fees.

ポイント：文の中心要素と修飾（分詞）部分の識別

2) （　　）内を適切な形に直して和訳しましょう。

❶ PART 5, (4)

Simply (write) with beautiful illustrations, the book is very popular.

ポイント：副詞的分詞（分詞構文）の形の決定と意味

❷ PART 5, (2)

The new scheme appears to be his (prefer) option.

ポイント：形容詞的分詞の形の決定

❸ PART 5, (6)

One of the (excite) developments in biology over the past few years has been the identification of the specific genes to cause cancer.

ポイント：形容詞的分詞の決定と主要素を見つけながらの和訳

3) （　　）から適切な形を選び和訳しましょう。

PART 5, (5)

I made my subordinates (talking / talked / talk) about the future plan of their business.

ポイント：使役動詞の目的語補語の形の決定

Unit 6 頻出 Words & Phrases

	W&P	発音	意味	Tips
☐1	**in large quantities**		⑦ 大量に	= in quantity
☐2	**goods**	/gúdz/	名 商品	
☐3	**slightly**	/sláɪtli/	副 少し	
☐4	**reduced**	/rɪdjúːst/	形 下がった	⑦ reduced price 値下げ価格
☐5	**be subject to**		⑦ ～に従っている	
☐6	**exceed**	/ɪksíːd/	動 ～を超える	形 excessive　過度の
☐7	**inspect**	/ɪnspékt/	動 ～を調査する	名 inspection 調査
☐8	**development**	/dɪvéləpmənt/	名 発展；開発	動 develop
☐9	**specific**	/spəsífɪk/	形 特定の	
☐10	**identification**	/aɪdèntɪfɪkéɪʃ(ə)n/	名 (身元) 確認	動 identify
☐11	**prefer**	/prɪfə́ːr/	動 ～をより好む	形 preferred 好ましい 副 preferably 希望を言えば
☐12	**confirm**	/kənfə́ːrm/	動 ～を確認する	名 confirmation 確認
☐13	**facility**	/fəsíləti/	名 施設；設備	
☐14	**patronage**	/péitr(ə)nɪdʒ/	名 ご愛顧	
☐15	**establishment**	/ɪstǽblɪʃmənt/	名 施設；建物	動 establish (→Unit 10)
☐16	**charge**	/tʃɑːrdʒ/	名 動 料金/請求する	⑦ be in charge of ～を担当する
☐17	**upcoming**	/ʌ́pkʌ̀mɪŋ/	形 間もなく起こる	
☐18	**participant**	/pərtísɪp(ə)nt/	名 参加者	★語尾注意
☐19	**recognize**	/rékəgnàɪz/	動 認める	名 recognition
☐20	**department**	/dɪpɑ́ːrtmənt/	名 部署	= division
☐21	**deadline**	/dédlàɪn/	名 締め切り	
☐22	**inclusive of**		⑦ ～を入れて	動 include
☐23	**cash register**		⑦ レジ	= cashier
☐24	**allow**	/əláu/	動 ～を許す	⑦ allow 人 to V 人が V するのを許す
☐25	**registration**	/rèdʒɪstréɪʃ(ə)n/	名 登録	動 register (→Unit 4)
☐26	**subordinate**	/səbɔ́ːrdɪnət/	名 部下	⇔ supervisor 上司 (→Unit 5)
☐27	**bureau**	/bjúərou/	名 事務所	
☐28	**retailer**	/ríːtèɪlər/	名 小売業者	
☐29	**recruit**	/rɪkrúːt/	名 新入社員	動 新規採用する
☐30	**on the premises**		⑦ 敷地内で	

Unit 7 前置詞

基本問題

① 類義の前置詞と接続詞の決め方は？

The country is becoming poor ------- a lack of natural resources.

(A) because　　(B) as　　(C) because of　　(D) owing

② 前置詞表現を正確に覚え選択しましょう。

The new leaflet on tax duty was published ------- taxpayer needs.

(A) prior to　　(B) in spite of　　(C) in response to　　(D) along with

③ 前置詞のイメージをもとに適切な前置詞を選択しましょう。

The institute will achieve a national and international reputation ------- excellence.

(A) with　　(B) in　　(C) at　　(D) for

Unit 7 で押さえる文法のルール

Rule 19　前置詞と接続詞の文法的な違い

品詞	後続する形	具体例		
		「〜だが」	「〜の間」	「〜のため」
前置詞	名詞（相当語句）**	despite, in spite of	during, for	because of, owing to
接続詞 *	文（S＋V … .)	(al)though	while	because, as, since

注：* 等位接続詞以外。　** 動名詞も含む。

【2語以上からなる前置詞表現（複合前置詞）】

● 「〜に答えて」：in response to
● 「〜のとき」：in the event of
● 「〜に一致して」：in accordance with
● 「〜の代わりに」：instead of, on behalf of
● 「〜に関して」：with/in regard to, as for, regarding
● 「〜現在」：as of
● 「〜に加えて」：in addition to, along with
● 「〜に従って・基づき」：according to, based on

in
[absorbed]

内部

on
[impose]

接触

with
[consistent, compete]

同伴・対立

over
[look, take]

覆う

into
[get, turn]

内部へ・変化

from / out of
[come, prevent]

外への起点・分離

to
[aim, related]

目的・到達

for
[apply, qualified]

方向・基準

through
[travel]

通過

PART 5 (短文穴埋め問題) の演習

ポイント □ルールを意識しながら問題を解く　□分からない語句にチェック　□文意の確認

1. ------- Thomas owned the property for a few years, he never lived there.
   - (A) Regardless of
   - (B) Although
   - (C) Since
   - (D) As a result of

2. Both automatic teller machines were fixed ------- the manufacturers' instructions.
   - (A) as to
   - (B) along with
   - (C) according to
   - (D) except for

3. All comments should be submitted ------- Tuesday 15 August 2017.
   - (A) until
   - (B) through
   - (C) to
   - (D) by

4. All redemptions of government stock are executed ------- the government by the Bank of England.
   - (A) on behalf of
   - (B) by reason of
   - (C) by means of
   - (D) on account of

5. The small company has benefited greatly ------- its low overheads.
   - (A) since
   - (B) from
   - (C) to
   - (D) for

6. In the West, business is sometimes discussed ------- lunch in people's homes.
   - (A) over
   - (B) above
   - (C) about
   - (D) within

7. I would not want to sit ------- a desk all day.
   - (A) in
   - (B) at
   - (C) on
   - (D) to

8. They express their concerns and expectations ------- the new suggestion.
   - (A) regarding
   - (B) in the event of
   - (C) as of
   - (D) by way of

9. He is keen to do a deal ------- investors who wish to achieve a greater return.
   - (A) with
   - (B) into
   - (C) as
   - (D) to

10. Many new recruits have been influenced by their experiences ------- a hospital stay or visit.
    - (A) while
    - (B) for
    - (C) at
    - (D) during

Notes: □ redemption 払い戻し

PART 1 （写真描写問題）の演習 34 ～ 35

1.

Ⓐ　Ⓑ　Ⓒ　Ⓓ

2.

Ⓐ　Ⓑ　Ⓒ　Ⓓ

PART 2 （応答問題）の演習 36 ～ 38

3. Mark your answer on your answer sheet.　　Ⓐ　Ⓑ　Ⓒ

4. Mark your answer on your answer sheet.　　Ⓐ　Ⓑ　Ⓒ

5. Mark your answer on your answer sheet.　　Ⓐ　Ⓑ　Ⓒ

ディクテイションにチャレンジ！

Part 1 🎧34 ～ 🎧35

1. A: One of the cushions is being placed _____.

   B: One of the tables is placed _____.

   C: The tables are placed _____.

   D: The sofas are arranged _____.

2. A: A man _____ the whiteboard.

   B: The computer _____ one woman.

   C: Everybody is sitting _____ one man.

   D: Two people are sitting at the table while _____

   _____.

Part 2 🎧36 ～ 🎧38

3. _____? _____.

   A: _____ when traffic is heavy.

   B: Drive _____, and _____.

   C: _____? _____ Ben's.

4. _____ before boarding the plane?

   A: _____ after you board the plane.

   B: To the check-in counter, _____.

   C: It's _____.

5. The weather report says _____ this weekend.

   A: But _____.

   B: Then _____.

   C: _____.

PART 6 (長文穴埋め問題) の演習

Questions 1-4 refer to the following notice.

Thank you for purchasing a Metcalf All-Terrain camping backpack! These bags are known ------- their durable and waterproof material as well as their easy access
1.
compartments. ------- other bags, Metcalf All-Terrain camping backpacks feature
2.
removable compartment dividers and an adjustable hidden pocket for valuables. They are the perfect bag for camping in the woods or moving from hostel to hostel on a European tour. Please read the warranty ------- before using your bag for the
3.
first time. -------. Please don't hesitate to contact us with any questions or comments
4.
at 269-555-2251.

1. (A) with
   (B) in
   (C) and
   (D) for

2. (A) Comparing
   (B) Unlike
   (C) Restricting
   (D) Excluding

3. (A) quickly
   (B) regularly
   (C) slowly
   (D) carefully

4. (A) We have customer service representatives always ready to assist you.
   (B) We have been in business for 54 years.
   (C) Write a review about our bag on our Web site.
   (D) Express delivery can be arranged for an extra fee.

Notes: ☐ compartment 小物入れ   ☐ warranty 保証書

PART 7 (読解問題) の演習

Questions 1-3 refer to the following form and letter.

The Manhattan University is one of the largest and most diverse institutions in New York with around 9,000 staff working in a wide range of academic, professional, technical and social roles.

Our staff have come from across the world to work with us, not only because of our outstanding academic reputation, but also because of the culture of innovation and forward thinking that is part of the way of life at Manhattan.

If you are interested in working with us, please submit your application form by June 20, according to one of the options below:

1. Submit your application form on our secure website: www.manhattan.edu.
2. Fax your application form to 1234-5678.
3. Send an e-mail including your application form to Hiro Tanaka at the Department of Human Resources (jobapplication@manhattan.edu).

As an alternative way to submit, please complete the form below and mail it with your application form to: The Manhattan University, 59 Church Street, New York, USA, 1234.

Name:

Address:

E-mail:

Telephone:

July 15, 2013

Dear Mr. Tanaka,

I mailed my application form to the designated postal address two weeks before the deadline, but I have not received any reply yet. Fortunately, I received a job offer from another university last night.

I would be very grateful if you could inform me of the results of my application ASAP. I am very interested in working for your university. However, I may have no option but to cancel my application if I do not hear from you very soon.

Sincerely,

Makoto Sakai

1. How did Mr. Sakai send his application form to the university?
(A) On the Web site
(B) By fax
(C) By e-mail
(D) By post

2. Why did Mr. Sakai write a letter to the university?
(A) He thought that the university was temporarily closed.
(B) He found that some information in his application needed to be changed.
(C) He was rejected by the university.
(D) He was not informed about the result of his application.

3. When did Mr. Sakai send his application form to the university?
(A) June 1
(B) June 6
(C) July 1
(D) Not mentioned

前置詞の練習

1) PART 6 の内容を思い出しながら、以下の空欄に適切な前置詞を選択肢から選びなさい。なお、選択肢の前置詞は、文頭にくるものも小文字で表記されています。

Thank you for purchasing a Metcalf All-Terrain camping backpack! These bags are known (　　　) their durable and waterproof material as well as their easy access compartments. (　　　) other bags, Metcalf All-Terrain camping backpacks feature removable compartment dividers and an adjustable hidden pocket for valuables. They are the perfect bag for camping in the woods or moving (　　　) hostel (　　　) hostel (　　　) a European tour. Please read the warranty carefully before using your bag for the first time. We have customer service representatives always ready to assist you. Please don't hesitate to contact us with any questions or comments (　　　) 269-555-2251.

　　選択肢： at　　for　　from　　on　　to　　unlike

2) 以下の日本語とほぼ同じ意味になるように英語で表現しなさい。前置詞の用法・表現に注意。

❶ 我々と働く（work with）ことに興味があれば、今月末までに願書をご提出ください。Part 7

　　If _____ .

❷ その機械は製造者の指示（manufacturers' instruction）に従って修理されている最中です。PART 5, (2)

　　_____

　　_____ .

❸ 私は請求書（invoice）を指定された住所に 2 週間前に郵送いたしました。Part 7

　　_____ .

❹ 彼は有名な投資家と取引（deal）をしたがっている（be keen to）。PART 5, (9)

　　_____ .

❺ 彼女のナイフとフォークは何もないお皿に並べて置かれています。Part 1

　　_____ .

	W&P	発音	意味	Tips
☐1	**regardless of**		⑦ ～に関わらず	＝despite（→Unit 5）
☐2	**own**	/óun/	動 ～を所有する	形 自分自身の
☐3	**property**	/prá(:)pərti/	名 不動産；財産	
☐4	**automatic**	/ɔ̀:təmǽtɪk/	形 自動の	
☐5	**temporarily**	/tèmpərér(ə)li/	副 一時的に	
☐6	**manufacturer**	/mæ̀njəfǽktʃ(ə)rər/	名 製造業者	名 動 manufacture（→Unit 8）
☐7	**durable**	/djúərəb(ə)l/	形 長持ちする；耐久力のある	
☐8	**except for**		⑦ ～を除いて	
☐9	**by means of**		⑦ ～の方法で	
☐10	**on account of**		⑦ ～のために	＝owing to ／ due to（→Unit 4）
☐11	**benefit**	/bénɪfɪt/	動 利益を得る	⑦ benefit O from … …から O を得る
☐12	**along with**		⑦ ～と一緒に	
☐13	**on behalf of**		⑦ ～の代わりに、～を代表して	
☐14	**expectation**	/èkspektéɪʃ(ə)n/	名 期待	動 expect 予期・期待する
☐15	**investor**	/ɪnvéstər/	名 投資家	動 invest (in)（～に）投資する 名 investment 投資
☐16	**achieve**	/ətʃíːv/	動 ～を達成する	名 achievement 達成
☐17	**influence**	/ínfluəns/	動 ～に影響を与える	形 influential 影響力のある
☐18	**designated**	/dézɪgnèɪtɪd/	形 指定された	
☐19	**side by side**		⑦ 並んで；一緒に	
☐20	**warranty**	/wɔ́:r(ə)nti/	名 保証（書）	＝guarantee
☐21	**adjustable**	/ədʒʌ́stəb(ə)l/	形 調整・適応できる	動 adjust ～を調整する 名 adjustment 修正・調整
☐22	**diverse**	/daɪvə́:rs/	形 多様化した	名 diversity 多様性
☐23	**institution**	/ìnstɪtjúːʃ(ə)n/	名 機関	
☐24	**reputation**	/rèpjətéɪʃ(ə)n/	名 名声；評判	
☐25	**outstanding**	/àʊtstǽndɪŋ/	形 顕著な	
☐26	**innovation**	/ìnəvéɪʃ(ə)n/	名 革新	形 innovative 革新的な
☐27	**hesitate**	/hézɪtèɪt/	動 躊躇する	⑦ do not hesitate to V ためらわず V する
☐28	**alternative**	/ɔːltə́:rnətɪv/	形 代わりの、別の	副 alternatively 代わりに
☐29	**complete**	/kəmplíːt/	動 ～を仕上げる	名 completion 完成
☐30	**board**	/bɔ́:rd/	動 に乗り込む／ 名 掲示板	⑦ on board に乗って

Unit 8 関係詞・接続詞

基本問題

① 関係詞の決定方法とは？

This summer I'll travel to Wellington, ------- is the capital of New Zealand.

(A) which

(B) that

(C) where

(D) whose

② 従属接続詞の選択とは？

She suffered complications ------- her blood pressure became unstable.

(A) providing

(B) if

(C) despite

(D) because

③ 等位接続詞を含むフレーズが主語に来た場合と動詞の選択とは？

Neither my client nor I ------- any approach to the company.

(A) has made

(B) have been made

(C) has to make

(D) have made

Rule 21 関係詞の選択手順

① 先行詞の種類を確認

先行詞	人	もの	場所	時間	理由	方法	"含む"
関係詞	who(m)	which	where	when	why	how	what
	所有格では whose						

注：目的格の関係詞は省略が可能。

② "完全な文"を従える関係詞か"不完全な文"を従える関係詞か

不完全な文を従える関係詞	完全な文を従える関係詞
who(m)/which/what/that	whose/where/when/how/why/ 前置詞 ＋ 不完全な関係詞 *

注：*"前置詞 ＋that"は定型表現 (in that) 以外なし。
　　-ever の複合関係詞も、-ever のない関係詞と同じ分類が適用される。

Rule 22 代表的な従属接続詞と従える節の種類

	whether	when	unless	as, since など	so that
名詞節	～かどうか（＝ if）	いつ～か	×	×	×
副詞節	～であろうとなかろうと	～のとき	～ないなら	～なので	～ために

Rule 23 等位接続詞を含む注意すべきフレーズ　＊A、B には同じ形（品詞）の語句

フレーズ	意味	フレーズが主語の場合の動詞の数
(both) A and B	A と B 両方	複数形扱い
([n]either) A [n]or B	A も B も [ない]	B に一致
(not only) A but (also) B	A だけでなく B も	B に一致
A as well as B	B はもちろん A も	A に一致

PART 5 (短文穴埋め問題)の演習

ポイント □ルールを意識しながら問題を解く　□分からない語句にチェック　□文意の確認

1. The plant, ------- will manufacture 100 vehicles a day, will begin operations soon.
   - (A) that
   - (B) who
   - (C) where
   - (D) which

2. We would like to thank those ------- took the time to participate in our event.
   - (A) when
   - (B) people
   - (C) ourselves
   - (D) who

3. ------- you place an order, you can view its status online.
   - (A) Once
   - (B) Although
   - (C) While
   - (D) Unless

4. Solid wastes are ------- burnt or buried in landfills.
   - (A) between
   - (B) neither
   - (C) both
   - (D) either

5. ------- matters in business is the personal relationships within the structure.
   - (A) Which
   - (B) That
   - (C) What
   - (D) One

6. ------- we look at children's writing, it is a priority to respond to the content.
   - (A) Whoever
   - (B) Whatever
   - (C) Whenever
   - (D) Whichever

7. Not only the type of soil but also its condition ------- the growth of plants in the ground.
   - (A) influence
   - (B) influences
   - (C) influential
   - (D) to influence

8. ------- the skill of conveying the exact meaning of messages to patients is vital to a nurse, it must be developed by clinical teachers.
   - (A) Owing to
   - (B) Although
   - (C) Besides
   - (D) As

9. All resources used must be monitored ------- project progress can be compared with the plan.
   - (A) there
   - (B) so that
   - (C) which
   - (D) in

10. ------- the recession is resolved swiftly, the market will remain uncertain for some time.
   - (A) If
   - (B) In the event that
   - (C) Unless
   - (D) The moment that

PART 2 (応答問題)の演習   40 ~ 42

1. Mark your answer on your answer sheet. Ⓐ Ⓑ Ⓒ

2. Mark your answer on your answer sheet. Ⓐ Ⓑ Ⓒ

3. Mark your answer on your answer sheet. Ⓐ Ⓑ Ⓒ

PART 4 (説明文問題)の演習 43

4. Who most likely is the listener?
   (A) A person who wants to be a plumber
   (B) A person who wants to be a travel planner
   (C) A person who wants to be an animation creator
   (D) A person who wants to be an estate agent

5. Which of the buttons should the listener press to take a trial lesson?
   (A) 1
   (B) 2
   (C) 3
   (D) 4

6. What information can current students get on the phone?
   (A) The TV program
   (B) The Inquiry Department
   (C) The name of teaching staff
   (D) The class cancellations

ディクテイションにチャレンジ！

Part 2 🎧40 ～ 🎧42

1. Do you know _____ report _____?

    A: _____.

    B: _____ last week.

    C: You can send _____.

2. _____?

    A: I _____ description.

    B: It _____ May 5th.

    C: The theater _____ from here.

3. I'm worried _____ be behind schedule.

    A: _____ train ride?

    B: Then _____.

    C: Yes, _____ 40 minutes.

シャドウイング＆オーバーラッピングにチャレンジ！

Part 4 🎧43

★ 「連結」「脱落」「同化」など音声変化に気を付けながら、音声を聞き、まずは後について発音してみましょう。次に、音声と同じスピードで発音してみましょう。発音と一緒に意味もとりながら挑戦してみましょう。

Thank you for calling TY Animation_Academy, a school for potential creators to learn basic skills for designing, programming, an(d) creating animate(d) movies. According to the following oral guidance, press_a button on your phone for the information you would like to know. For details_of our academy and our courses, please press one. For students who are interested_in_a trial lesson, press two. For curren(t) students, press three to check_on the cancellation_of classes. An(d) for any other information, pre(ss) seven to tal(k) to the Inquiry Departmen(t) staff. Thank you for your call. Create animation for your future!!

PART 6 (長文穴埋め問題) の演習

Questions 1-3 refer to the following e-mail.

To:	Stephen Murray <murray@icttechnoservice.com>
From:	Clark G. Williams <clark_williams@bigslope.com>
Subject:	New project

Dear Mr. Murray,

Thank you for your email on the 1st of July. I am very satisfied with the technical system ------- clearly shows the process of converting standard issued
1.
books into an electronically available format. In addition, I am certainly interested in the possibility of your collaboration and assistance in our work on the electronic publishing project and would be glad to meet you to discuss this. -------.
2.
-------, I am tied up for the next month, but I hope we can arrange a time in
3.
September. If you phone my secretary, Shirley Ballard, at ------- 5065, I am sure
4.
she will be able to sort everything out.

Yours truly,

Clark G. Williams

Chief Editor, Bigslope Publishing Company

1. (A) there
   (B) what
   (C) which
   (D) where

2. (A) She has been involved in the publishing project.
   (B) I would like you to give me further advice about any technical applications.
   (C) I will have a plenty of time to discuss it next month.
   (D) Such collaboration and assistance are not what I have hoped.

3. (A) Conveniently
   (B) Economically
   (C) Strictly
   (D) Unfortunately

4. (A) admission
   (B) caption
   (C) extension
   (D) intention

PART 7 (読解問題) の演習

Questions 1-4 refer to the following statement and memo.

Expense Account Statement

Employee: Akira Tada

For period ending: Oct/10/2013

Reimbursable Expenses Incurred

[Accommodation]	[Transportation]
Hotel (New York) $800.00	Air $970.00
Hotel (Los Angeles) $150.00	Train $48.00
	Bus $16.00
[Meals]	Taxi $51.00
Lunch $100.00	
Dinner $200.00	**Total: $2335.00**

Receipts are attached to this form.

Signature : *Akira Tada*

To: Akira Tada

From: Miyoko Sakai, A/P

Dear Mr. Tada,

Your submitted expense account statement indicates that an amount spent on hotels exceeds the company's expenses limit. The standard reimbursement allowance is $150 per night, so your stay in New York for 4 nights is over the limit. For this reason, I require you to submit another form for reimbursement beyond the standard allowable expenses by November 10th if you wish to be reimbursed fully for your accommodation expenses.

Regards,

Miyoko Sakai

---

1. Why did Mr. Tada submit the statement?
   (A) To submit the receipts for transportation
   (B) To book his air ticket
   (C) To make a hotel reservation
   (D) To request repayment for all travel costs

2. Which expenditure went over the company limit?
   (A) Transportation
   (B) Tax
   (C) Accommodation
   (D) Meals

Notes: □ expense account statement：所用経費報告書　□ A/P (Account Payable)：買掛金勘定

3. How long did Mr. Tada stay at the hotel in New York?
(A) Two nights
(B) Three nights
(C) Four nights
(D) Five nights

4. By how much did the expenses account exceed the reimbursement allowance?
(A) $100
(B) $200
(C) $300
(D) $400

関係詞・接続詞の練習

1) 以下の各英文を関係詞・接続詞用法に注意しながら和訳しましょう。

❶ The plant, which will manufacture 100 vehicles a day, will begin operations soon.
PART 5, (1)

_____

❷ We would like to thank those who took the time to participate in our event.
PART 5, (2)

_____

❸ What matters in business is the personal relationships within the structure.
PART 5, (5)

_____

❹ All resources used must be monitored so that project progress can be compared with the plan. PART 5, (9)

_____

2) 適切な接続詞を使って英語で表現してみましょう。

❶ 一度、注文をすると、状況はオンラインで確認できます。PART 5, (3)

_____

❷ 契約を交わす（sign）時はいつでも、契約内容（the agreement）を吟味することが優先事項です。PART 5, (6)

_____

❸ 製品の質（product quality）だけでなく経済状況（economic situation）もその年の売り上げに影響を及ぼします。PART 5, (7)

_____

❹ 大学の場所とバスのルートがのっている地図がここにあります。PART 6 応用

_____

Unit 8　頻出 Words & Phrases 🎧44

	W&P	発音	意味	Tips
☐1	**convert**	/kənvə́:rt/	動 〜を変換する	⑦ convert A into B A を B に変える
☐2	**sort out**		⑦ 〜を手配する	
☐3	**collaboration**	/kəlæ̀bəréɪʃ(ə)n/	名 協力	動 collaborate (+with) 〜と協力する
☐4	**assistance**	/əsíst(ə)ns/	名 援助	動 assist 〜を援助する
☐5	**electronically**	/ɪlèktrá(:)nɪk(ə)li/	副 電子的に	形 electronic 電子の
☐6	**unfortunately**	/ʌnfɔ́:rtʃ(ə)nətli/	副 不運にも	
☐7	**expense**	/ɪkspéns/	名 費用；経費	≒ expenditure ⑦ at own expense 自費で
☐8	**extension**	/ɪksténʃ(ə)n/	動 内線、延長	形 extensive 広範囲にわたる
☐9	**incur**	/ɪnkə́:r/	動 負う	
☐10	**reimbursement**	/rì:ɪmbə́:rsmənt/	名 払い戻し	動 reimburse 払い戻す 形 reimbursable
☐11	**in the event that**		⑦ 〜する場合には	
☐12	**detail**	/dí:teɪl/	名 詳細	⑦ in more detail より詳しく
☐13	**behind schedule**		⑦ 予定より遅れて	⇔ ahead of schedule 予定より進んで
☐14	**on time**		⑦ 時間通り	⑦ in time 間に合って
☐15	**estate agent**		⑦ 不動産業者	= real-estate agent
☐16	**satisfied**	/sǽtɪsfàɪd/	動 満足した	⑦ be satisfied with〜 〜に満足している
☐17	**plant**	/plænt/	名 工場、植物	
☐18	**status**	/stéɪtəs/	名 状況	
☐19	**participate in**		⑦ 〜に参加する	= join / take part in
☐20	**manufacture**	/mæ̀njəfǽktʃər/	動 〜を製造する	名 manufacturing 製造
☐21	**respond**	/rɪspá(:)nd/	動 〜に応える (+to)	名 response 返答、反応
☐22	**priority**	/praɪɔ́:rəti/	名 優先（事項）	
☐23	**content**	/ká(:)ntent/	名 内容	
☐24	**vital**	/váɪt(ə)l/	形 極めて重要な	= essential / crucial (→Unit 11)
☐25	**resource**	/rí:sɔ:rs /	名 資源	形 resourceful 資源に富んだ
☐26	**monitor**	/má(:)nətər/	動 〜を監視する	
☐27	**compare**	/kəmpéər/	動 〜を比較する	名 comparison 比較 形 comparable 比較できる
☐28	**resolve**	/rɪzá(:)lv/	動 〜を解決する	
☐29	**secretary**	/sékrətèri/	名 秘書	
☐30	**description**	/dɪskrípʃ(ə)n/	名 説明、描写	⑦ beyond description 言葉にできない

Unit 9 助動詞と仮定法

基本問題

① **助動詞の基本用法と紛らわしい表現とは？**

In order to be able to help effectively, we ------- to hold personal information on file.

　(A) should

　(B) need

　(C) cannot

　(D) need not

② **仮定法の基本的な形とは？**

If I ------- you, I would be looking around a bit.

　(A) had been

　(B) am

　(C) were

　(D) be

③ **仮定法現在における注意点とは？**

TTN shareholders are demanding that the highest bidder, CTV, ------- their intended stakes from 20% to 15%.

　(A) to cut

　(B) is cutting

　(C) cuts

　(D) cut

Unit 9 で押さえる文法のルール

Rule 24　注意が必要な基本助動詞の用法

表現	意味	表現	意味
cannot V	V するはずがない	do not have to V	V する必要がない
must not V	V してはならない	used to [would] V	かつて V だった [した]
should have Vp.p.	すべきだったのに（しなかった）	need* not have Vp.p. * 動詞では need to V	V する必要がなかったのに

注：助動詞を単純に過去形にしても過去の内容を示さない（could V [V できた] は例外）。

Rule 25 仮定法過去・過去完了・現在の形式と仮定法を含むフレーズ

仮定法の種類	形式 & 意味
仮定法過去 （反現実）	If S' + *V'p*., S + 助動詞の過去形 + V 「もし S' が V' なら、S は V であろうに」
仮定法過去完了 （過去の反事実）	If S' + *had* + V'p.p., S + 助動詞の過去形 + have + Vp.p. 「もし S' が V' であったなら、S は V であったろうに」
仮定法現在 （実現の低い推量）	If S' + *should* [*were to*]V', S + 助動詞の過去形 [will] + V 「万一 S' が V' ならば、S は V であろう」

注：if を省略し、倒置が可能。その場合、イタリック部分が文頭に移動。

【仮定法を含むフレーズ】

● as if S' + V'p/had Vp.p.：まるで S' が V' のように / だったように
　＊仮定法過去か過去完了を用いるかどうかは、主節との時間の差で決定 **Rule 12**

● if it were not for / if it had not been for：〜がなければ / 〜がなかったら

● without / but for：〜がなければ・なかったら　⇔　with：〜があれば・あったら

● it is (about/high) time that S' + V'p：（そろそろ / とっくに）V' する時間だ

● had better V：V したほうがいい

● would rather V：むしろ V したい

Rule 26 仮定法現在を従える「要求・提案」の動詞・形容詞・名詞

「要求・提案」の意味の語句 ＋ that S' (should) V' の原形 .... .

動　詞：demand（要求する）　　require（要求する）　　　　order（命令する）
　　　　advise（忠告する）　　　suggest（提案する）　　　　propose（提案する）
　　　　recommend（勧める）など

形容詞：necessary（必要だ）　　imperative（絶対必要だ）　desirable（望ましい）
　　　　advisable（賢明だ）　　　essential（必要不可欠だ）など

名　詞：request（要請；依頼）　suggestion（提案）　　　　demand（要求）など

PART 5（短文穴埋め問題）の演習

ポイント □ルールを意識しながら問題を解く　□分からない語句にチェック　□文意の確認

1. If we are designing a product, we ------- to be aware of the viewpoint of the consumers.
   - (A) should
   - (B) had better
   - (C) need
   - (D) must

2. We ------- something earlier to improve the situation, but we couldn't.
   - (A) should do
   - (B) would rather do
   - (C) should have done
   - (D) had done

3. If I asked for money from my husband, ------- of all the expenses.
   - (A) he would talk
   - (B) he talked
   - (C) he will talk
   - (D) he talk

4. If he -------, she would probably have joined him and discussed the solution with him.
   - (A) had success
   - (B) had not succeeded
   - (C) has not succeeded
   - (D) has success

5. I wish I ------- studied economics more when I was a student.
   - (A) have
   - (B) had
   - (C) could
   - (D) had been

6. A conclusion ------- include all information that you have presented: it may only be part of it.
   - (A) will
   - (B) must not
   - (C) not need to
   - (D) does not have to

7. ------- adequate insurance, repairing or replacing your belongings could be extremely expensive.
   - (A) With
   - (B) If it had not been for
   - (C) Without
   - (D) If there were not for

8. ------- a non-standard system, a full description will be available from the librarian.
   - (A) Should a library use
   - (B) A library uses
   - (C) Use a library
   - (D) Had a library used

9. She was advised that she ------- to try to reduce weight through her leg exercises.
   - (A) continues
   - (B) will continue
   - (C) should continue
   - (D) is continued

10. There is a suggestion that the brochure ------- once a year.
    - (A) is updating
    - (B) be updated
    - (C) updates
    - (D) will update

リスニング・セクション

PART 1（写真描写問題）の演習 🎧45 ~ 🎧46

1.

        Ⓐ   Ⓑ   Ⓒ   Ⓓ

2.

        Ⓐ   Ⓑ   Ⓒ   Ⓓ

PART 2（応答問題）の演習 🎧47 ~ 🎧49

3. Mark your answer on your answer sheet.   Ⓐ Ⓑ Ⓒ

4. Mark your answer on your answer sheet.   Ⓐ Ⓑ Ⓒ

5. Mark your answer on your answer sheet.   Ⓐ Ⓑ Ⓒ

Part 1 45 ~ 46

1. A: The skyscrapers _____.

   B: All _____.

   C: The statue _____.

   D: The architects _____ design.

2. A: The sign shows _____.

   B: People _____.

   C: The sign _____ the wall.

   D: No fines _____ the rules.

Part 2 47 ~ 49

3. _____.

   A: _____.

   B: _____.

   C: _____.

4. _____ without your help.

   A: _____.

   B: Sorry, _____.

   C: _____.

5. May I interrupt you for a moment or _____

   _____?

   A: _____. _____.

   B: _____ interpreter.

   C: _____.

リーディング・セクション

PART 6 (長文穴埋め問題) の演習

Questions 1-4 refer to the following memo.

Memorandum

From: Frank Becker

To: Ellen Steiner

Date: April 5

-------.
1.
I would like to know ------- else James wants as part of this deal. I feel that we
2.
should support his opening of the first agency in Asia whenever we can. I know
Emily Beckham, who he mentions is trying hard to push our musical instruments in
China, and ------- feel confident about her support. ------- satisfactory answer to my
3.   **4.**
first question, I would feel comfortable with allowing exclusivity on the market in
Beijing. I will offer a contract that allows him exclusivity if he gets a minimum of 150
distributors in October.

---

1. (A) A deal with James has been very successful.
(B) I have some inquiry about a recent deal.
(C) I would like you to notify all employees of the contract.
(D) There was no room for discussion on the campaign.

2. (A) that
(B) what
(C) which
(D) where

3. (A) rather than
(B) yet
(C) therefore
(D) alternatively

4. (A) I had
(B) Had been
(C) If I have
(D) Had I

Notes: ☐ exclusivity 独占権　☐ distributor 特約販売店

Questions 1-5 refer to the following review article and letter.

Review for the Walker B50

by David Anderson

The new product released from SONIC is an innovative compact audio player. The Walker B50 is a handy size, only 4.0-inches tall. With 200GB of storage, it can hold up to 80,000 songs, 400 hours of videos or 50,000 photos.

This device consists of a touch-screen panel. With a few taps, you can find exactly the songs or videos you want to listen to or watch in your library. On this magical touch-screen panel, you can adjust volume as well as tune dials for radio and TV channels. The B50 can also connect to the Internet through Wi-Fi.

Its design is so simple but it looks breathtakingly innovative, with its polished stainless steel catching the eye. This stylish device also has dual speakers at the bottom, sounding far better than anything else produced by the competition. Only available in white.

To: The Editor of New Goods Magazine

Thank you for your positive review of our new product. The concept of the Walker B50 is the fusion of modern technology and classic design, creating a user-friendly device for everyone. The target purchasers are people who care about both sound and looks.

Because of your positive review for our product, I am glad to inform you about an upcoming product. We will announce the new B60 version in a month. Two new colors, silver and gold, will be added to the current lineup.

Also, the B60 will come loaded with 12 games, including the card game Poker. The size of the display will be enlarged to 5.0-inches. Users will also be able to rent or purchase TV programs, movies and dramas. But best of all, the price will go down to just $50, half the price of the current one. You will be able to enjoy life with the B60 anytime, anywhere.

Sincerely,

Steven Sinclair

President, SONIC

Note: ☐ breathtakingly 息をのむような

1. Who is David Anderson?
   (A) A subscriber to the magazine
   (B) An appliance lover
   (C) An editor of a magazine
   (D) A developer of the B50

2. What is NOT a feature of the B50?
   (A) The white color
   (B) The stainless steel
   (C) The large amount of storage
   (D) The fingerprint authentication
      system

3. What is the main point of Mr. Sinclair's
   letter?
   (A) To give information about a new
      product
   (B) To review the current product
   (C) To apply for the job position
      announced by New Goods Magazine
   (D) To correct the information about the
      B50 in the review

4. How much is the B50?
   (A) $50
   (B) $100
   (C) $150
   (D) $200

5. What color variations will the B60
   have?
   (A) White only
   (B) Silver and gold
   (C) White, silver and gold
   (D) Not stated

❶ On this touch-screen panel, you can adjust volume as well as tune dials for radio and TV channels. PART 7

_____ .

ポイント：助動詞の意味・等位接続詞

❷ Should you be charged twice, please call at customer service and we will refund the extra charge. PART 5 応用

_____ .

ポイント：仮定法で用いられる助動詞と倒置・命令文＋and ～の構文

❸ Without adequate insurance, repairing your belongings could be extremely expensive. PART 5, (7)

_____ .

ポイント：条件表現・動名詞

英作文に挑戦

❶ そろそろ我が社もより厳しい禁煙政策を採用する（adopt）ときです。

_____ .

❷ 君に明確な回答を与えられれば良いのだけれど。

_____ .

❸ 予算を超えないように。〔imperative that を用いて〕

_____ .

❹ 少しお邪魔してもよろしいですか、それとも話が終わるまで待ちましょうか。

_____ .

Unit 9 頻出 Words & Phrases

	W&P	発音	意味	Tips
☐1	**permit**	/pərmít/	動 ～を許す	名 permission 許可
☐2	**fine**	/fáɪn/	名 罰金 形 すばらしい；晴れた	
☐3	**agency**	/éɪdʒ(ə)nsi/	名 代理店	句 travel agency 旅行代理店
☐4	**satisfactory**	/sæ̀tɪsfǽkt(ə)ri/	形 十分な	＝adequate
☐5	**distributor**	/dɪstríbjətər/	名 流通業者	名 特約販売店
☐6	**release**	/rilíːs/	名 動 発売・発表 （する）	句 press release 報道資料
☐7	**storage**	/stɔ́ːrɪdʒ/	名 貯蔵、容量	動 名 store ～を蓄える / お店
☐8	**polished**	/pá(ː)lɪʃt/	形 磨かれた	動 polish ～を磨く
☐9	**device**	/dɪváɪs/	名 装置	
☐10	**skyscraper**	/skáɪskrèɪpər/	名 超高層ビル	
☐11	**minimum**	/mínɪməm/	名 形 最低限（の）	⇔ maximum 最大限（の）
☐12	**impose**	/ɪmpóʊz/	動 ～を課す	句 impose A on/upon B A を B に課す
☐13	**attach**	/ətǽtʃ/	動 ～を取り付ける	句 attached file 添付ファイル
☐14	**architect**	/ɑ́ːrkɪtèkt/	名 建築家	
☐15	**economics**	/ìːkəná(ː)mɪks/	名 経済学	
☐16	**update**	/ʌ̀pdéɪt/	動 情報を更新する	形 updated 更新された
☐17	**exclusivity**	/ɪkskluːsívəti/	名 独占権	副 exclusively
☐18	**advise**	/ədváɪz/	動 助言する；勧める	名 advice 助言
☐19	**replace**	/ripléɪs/	動 ～を取り換える	名 replacement 交替；代用品
☐20	**repair**	/ripéər/	動 ～を修理する	＝fix
☐21	**insurance**	/ɪnʃúər(ə)ns/	名 保険	
☐22	**viewpoint**	/vjúːpɔ̀ɪnt/	名 視点；観点	
☐23	**belongings**	/bɪlɔ́ːŋɪŋz/	名 所有物	
☐24	**consumer**	/kənsjúːmər/	名 消費者	動 consume ～を消費する 名 consumption 消費
☐25	**product**	/prá(ː)dʌkt/	名 製品	名 production 生産 動 produce ～を生産する
☐26	**include**	/ɪnklúːd/	動 ～を含む	前 including 含めて
☐27	**information**	/ìnfərméɪʃ(ə)n/	名 情報	形 informative 情報に富む
☐28	**conclusion**	/kənklúːʒ(ə)n/	名 結論	動 conclude 結論付ける
☐29	**be aware of**		句 ～に気づいている	
☐30	**current**	/kə́ːr(ə)nt/	形 現在の	副 currently 現在（のところ）

Unit 10　比較とTOEIC®頻出の形容詞

基本問題

① 比較の基本的な考え方と構文を確認しましょう

The job of the share analyst is ------- of the bond analyst.

    (A) more difficult than

    (B) the most difficult than

    (C) more difficult than that

    (D) as difficult than that

② TOEIC でよく出題される形容詞を押さえましょう

It is hard to persuade interviewers that you have ------- skills if you have been out of office for years.

    (A) frequent

    (B) managerial

    (C) steady

    (D) indicative

③ 数えられる（可算）名詞と数えられない（不可算）名詞を修飾する大小の表現とは？

He had ------- money saved and he began to use it up.

    (A) few

    (B) a lot

    (C) a little

    (D) a great number of

Unit 10 で押さえる文法のルール

Rule 27　比較表現の基本形

	形式	意味
同等比較級	A as 形容詞 / 副詞の原級 as B	A は B と同じくらい…
比較級	A 形容詞 / 副詞の比較級 than B	A は B より…
最上級	A the 形容詞 / 副詞の最上級 in /of ～	A は～の中で最も…

注：A・B は文法的・意味的に同種類。一部の例外を除き、比較級は「形容詞 / 副詞の原級＋-er」、最上級は「the ＋形容詞 / 副詞の原級＋-est」。長い語の場合は、比較級は"more ＋ 形容詞 / 副詞の原級"、最上級は"the most ＋ 形容詞 / 副詞の原級"。

【比較級・最上級の強調表現】

【比較級】much ／（by）far ／（a）lot(s) ／ considerably

【最上級】by far ／ very

【比較級を含むフレーズ】

● the 比較級 A, the 比較級 B：「A すればするほど B」

● the 比較級 of（the）two〜：「2 つの〜のうち…の方」

＊比較級に the がつくことに注意

●倍数詞 as 〜 as A：「A の○倍〜で」

＊倍数詞は half, twice, three times . . .

● the ＋ 比較級 of（the）two 〜：「2 つの〜のうち…の方」

● superior to A：A より優れている ⇔ inferior to A：A より劣っている

● not more than：せいぜい（＝ at most）

● no more than：たった（＝ only）

● not less than：少なくとも（＝ at least）

● no less than：以上（＝ more than）

Rule 28 数量形容詞と可算・不可算名詞

	可算名詞	不可算名詞	不 / 可算名詞
多い	many / a great[large] number of	much / a great[large] amount[deal] of 〜	a lot of, lots of
少ない	a few (few ほとんど〜ない)	a little (little ほとんど〜ない)	

【金額を高低（high/low）で表す名詞】

income（収入）　　price（価格）　　salary（給料）　　tax*（税金）*big / small も可

ポイント □ルールを意識しながら問題を解く　□分からない語句にチェック　□文意の確認

1. Handwriting recognition is ------- than OCR due to the variety of handwriting styles among writers.
   - (A) very harder
   - (B) as harder
   - (C) much harder
   - (D) a little hard

2. The country has ------- proportion of heavy smokers among men in the world.
   - (A) higher
   - (B) as high
   - (C) highest
   - (D) the highest

3. Sales for publishing businesses have grown ------- as those for net businesses in the past three years.
   - (A) twice as faster
   - (B) ten as fast
   - (C) half as fast
   - (D) three times more fast

4. ------- you study about business administration, the more you understand how hard it is to run a company.
   - (A) The more
   - (B) The
   - (C) The most
   - (D) Better

5. ------- of the two chips fits in the main processor socket.
   - (A) Large
   - (B) The largest
   - (C) The larger
   - (D) The large

6. Joe is ------- to establish a more suitable and rewarding partnership.
   - (A) possible
   - (B) capable
   - (C) able
   - (D) feasible

7. The new project by Allen is ------- with his company's current policy.
   - (A) independent
   - (B) consistent
   - (C) eligible
   - (D) reliable

8. They were working but had only a ------- basic salary.
   - (A) much
   - (B) low
   - (C) light
   - (D) short

9. The product has been evaluated as very effective, so there are ------- a few complaints made about it each year.
   - (A) not less than
   - (B) no more than
   - (C) more than
   - (D) no less than

10. The company only has ------- money to invest in research and development at this time.
    - (A) many
    - (B) a few
    - (C) few
    - (D) a little

リスニング・セクション

PART 2 (応答問題) の演習 51 ~ 53

1. Mark your answer on your answer sheet. Ⓐ Ⓑ Ⓒ

2. Mark your answer on your answer sheet. Ⓐ Ⓑ Ⓒ

3. Mark your answer on your answer sheet. Ⓐ Ⓑ Ⓒ

PART 3 (会話問題) の演習 54

Dentist Business Hours	
Monday & Tuesday	9 am – 6 pm
Wednesday & Thursday	8 am – 4 pm
Friday	8 am – noon
*closed on weekends & holidays	

4. What is the main purpose of the call?
   (A) To check which holiday the dentist is closed
   (B) To find out where she can get the business card
   (C) To make an appointment with the dentist
   (D) To ask the open hours of the fitness club

5. What is the woman most likely to do next?
   (A) Tell the man her name
   (B) Close the office
   (C) Go to the dentist
   (D) Make a phone call

6. Look at the graphic. What day of the week did the woman call?
   (A) Monday
   (B) Tuesday
   (C) Thursday
   (D) Friday

Part 2 🎧51 ~ 🎧53

1. _____ hire?

    A: They work _____.

    B: I think _____.

    C: _____.

2. _____ a little earlier?

    A: Yes, we can. _____?

    B: _____.

    C: _____ there.

3. _____.

    A: _____, _____.

    B: _____?

    C: Yes, _____.

シャドウイング＆オーバーラッピングからのペアワークにチャレンジ！

Part 3

★「連結」「脱落」「同化」など音声変化に気を付けながら、音声を聞き、まずは後について発音してみましょう。次に、音声と同じスピードで発音してみましょう。発音と一緒に意味もとりながら挑戦してみましょう。

Woman: Hello. I'd li(ke) to schedule a dental check-up_a(t) 2 p.m. this_afternoon.

Man: Well Madam, we're closing in_an_hour today.

Woman: But it's_only 11_am now. Aren't you usually open till 4 or 6 p.m.?

Man: No. Our business_hours are 8_am to noon today. An(d) nex(t) Monday,
           we'll be closed for_a holiday.

Woman: Right! I jus(t) found your business hour(s) shown on the card . How abou(t)
            nex(t) Tuesday, in the afternoon, then?

Man: Yes, I can fit you in_on Tuesday, a(t) 3 in the afternoon. May I have your
           name, please?

リーディング・セクション

PART 6 (長文穴埋め問題) の演習

Questions 1-4 refer to the following press release.

Windsor, September 14 - Windsor Women's Center, the new complex ------- has
1.
more facilities for local women under one roof, will open professional and
educational courses.

The Women Returners course, which is for women ------- to get back into the
2.
workplace or further education, will start on Thursday October 14. The nine-week
project is to offer practical advice on application forms and CVs as well as
information on higher education options.

-------. This is WWC Open University course, which is designed for those
3.
considering higher education, ranging from sociology to creative writing. -------, it
4.
covers crafts and woodwork.

For those interested in the above courses, please visit our Web site,
www.windsorswomencenter.com, for updated and detailed information.

---

1. (A) what
   (B) which
   (C) there
   (D) where

2. (A) reluctant
   (B) keen
   (C) capable
   (D) skilled

3. (A) Access Course will also be starting on the same day.
   (B) The university will open several new courses.
   (C) Designing courses have been very popular.
   (D) The registration deadline for a new course was the other day.

4. (A) However
   (B) In summary
   (C) Instead
   (D) Furthermore

Notes: □ complex 複合施設　□ CVs（Curriculum Vitae）履歴書　□ craft 工芸　□ woodwork 木工

Questions 1-5 refer to the following invitation and e-mail.

Banquet Invitation

You are hereby cordially invited to attend a banquet to commemorate the final evening of this year's annual conference.

       Place: Main Ballroom

       Date: Sunday 15 November

       Time: 6 p.m. onwards

       RSVP: Friday 13 November

       Cost: $60 per person inclusive of full buffet (10% additional discount given for members)

       Alcoholic Beverages: At own expense

We look forward to seeing you there to celebrate the success of the conference.

Conference Committee Chairperson

Wednesday 11 November

OOO

Dear Professor Johnston,

It was a pleasure to have the opportunity to meet with you recently at this year's Annual Conference, following your keynote presentation. I spoke with a number of colleagues who were also equally impressed by your findings.

In fact, on behalf of the Vice-Chancellor, I would like to request your consideration, dependent of course on your availability and other commitments you may have, in visiting our campus at your convenience in order to address our graduate students, who I feel certain would also greatly benefit from your expertise in this field. Naturally, we would incur any transportation and accommodation costs that arise, but we would also like to remunerate you for your valuable time.

In the meantime, I would be most grateful for a copy of your recent publications from your in-house journal to peruse if I may.

Thank you in anticipation for your consideration. I look forward to hearing from you at your convenience and hopefully seeing you at this evening's final banquet.

Sincerely,

(Professor Dr) Paul Smith

Dean, Faculty of Foreign Studies

---

1. When is the deadline for responses regarding the banquet?
(A) Wednesday, November 11
(B) Friday, November 13
(C) Sunday, November 15
(D) Not stated

2. How much is the banquet?
(A) Free for all members
(B) $66 inclusive of buffet and drinks for non-members
(C) $54 for full buffet excluding drinks for members
(D) $60 regardless of whether the person attending is a member or not

3. What is the main purpose in the correspondence to Professor Johnston?
(A) To thank her for the speech she gave at the conference
(B) To request a copy of her recent research
(C) To enquire about her availability
(D) To invite her to speak at Professor Smith's campus to students

4. What payment is Professor Smith offering Professor Johnston?
(A) None, as it is a professional courtesy
(B) Hotel, transport and an additional payment for speaking
(C) Only transportation and accommodation
(D) All banquet costs

5. Where is Professor Smith likely to see Professor Johnston next time?
(A) At Professor Smith's university
(B) At this year's annual conference rooms
(C) In Professor Johnston's laboratory
(D) In the Main Ballroom

Notes: □ RSVP ご返答を請う　□ keynote presentation 基調講演　□ commitments 業務
□ remunerate 報酬を支払う

❶ On behalf of the Vice-Chancellor, I would like to request your consideration, dependent on your availability and other commitments you may have, in visiting our campus at your convenience in order to address our graduate students, who I feel certain would also greatly benefit from your expertise. PART 7, e-mail, *line* 4

ポイント：挿入部分と中心部分の判別、前置詞・形容詞表現

❷ The project is to offer practical advice on application forms and CVs as well as information on higher education options. PART 6, *line* 5

ポイント：比較表現と等位接続詞

❶ 危険な賭けをする（take risks）ほど、より多くの利益を得られそうだ。 PART 5, (4) 応用

❷ 腕のいい交渉人というのは、そうでない交渉人（the less skilled）と比べ少なくとも2倍は多くの質問をする。 PART 5, (3) 応用

❸ 彼はその新職に適任です。 PART 5, (7) 応用
　　□ eligible を用いて

Unit 10　頻出 Words & Phrases 55

	W&P	発音	意味	Tips
☐1	**at least**		㋹ 少なくとも	= not less than
☐2	**appoint<u>ment</u>**	/əpɔ́ɪntmənt/	㊢ 予約	㋹ make an appointment 予約をする
☐3	**check-up**		㊃ 健康診断；検査	
☐4	**professiona<u>l</u>**	/prəféʃ(ə)n(ə)l/	㊢ 職業の	㊃ profe<u>ssion</u>（専門的）職業
☐5	**regarding**	/rɪɡɑ́:rdɪŋ/	㊝ ～に関して	= concerning / as for / in[with] regard to
☐6	**opt<u>ion</u>**	/ɑ́(:)pʃ(ə)n/	㊃ 選択肢	
☐7	**craft**	/kræft/	㊃ 工芸	
☐8	**banquet**	/bǽŋkwət/	㊃ 祝宴	
☐9	**address**	/ədrés/	㊊ ～に演説する	㊃ 住所
☐10	**dependent**	/dɪpénd(ə)nt/	㊢ 頼っている	㋹ dependent on ⇔ independent of
☐11	**recogni<u>tion</u>**	/rèkəɡníʃ(ə)n/	㊃ 識別；認識	㊊ recog<u>nize</u> ～を認識する（→Unit 6）
☐12	**run**	/rʌn/	㊊ ～を経営する	
☐13	**admini<u>stration</u>**	/ədmìnɪstréɪʃ(ə)n/	㊃ 経営；管理	㊢ administra<u>tive</u> 管理/経営の
☐14	**establish**	/ɪstǽblɪʃ/	㊊ ～を設立する	㊃ establish<u>ment</u>
☐15	**suit<u>able</u>**	/sú:təb(ə)l/	㊢ 適した；向いた	
☐16	**reward<u>ing</u>**	/rɪwɔ́:rdɪŋ/	㊢ やりがいのある	㊃ reward 報酬（金）
☐17	**cap<u>able</u>**	/kéɪpəb(ə)l/	㊢ 能力のある	㋹ be capable of ……できる
☐18	**feas<u>ible</u>**	/fí:zəb(ə)l/	㊢ 実行可能な	㋹ S（人以外）be feasible to V
☐19	**in the correspon<u>dence</u> to ～**		㋹ ～に一致している	
☐20	**consis<u>tent</u>**	/kənsíst(ə)nt/	㊢ 一貫した	㋹ be consistent with … …と一貫している
☐21	**reli<u>able</u>**	/rɪlá(ɪ)əb(ə)l/	㊢ 信頼できる	㊃ reliabili<u>ty</u> 信頼（性） ㊊ rely（+ on）～に頼る
☐22	**salary**	/sǽl(ə)ri/	㊃ 給料	
☐23	**evaluate**	/ɪvǽljuèɪt/	㊊ ～を評価する	㊃ evalua<u>tion</u> 評価
☐24	**complaint**	/kəmpléɪnt/	㊃ 不平；不満	㊊ complain（+ about）～について不平を言う
☐25	**meantime**	/mí:ntàɪm/	㊃ その間	㋹ in the meantime その間は
☐26	**dean**	/di:n/	㊃ 学部長	
☐27	**expertise**	/èkspəːrtí:z/	㊃ 専門知識	
☐28	**commemor<u>ate</u>**	/kəmémərèɪt/	㊊ ～を祝う	㊃ commemora<u>tion</u> 祝賀
☐29	**availabili<u>ty</u>**	/əvèɪləbíləti/	㊃ 都合	
☐30	**propor<u>tion</u>**	/prəpɔ́:rʃ(ə)n/	㊃ 割合	

基本問題

① 数えられる（可算）名詞と数えられない（不可算）名詞とは？

------- of the latest technology is very little.

(A) A knowledge

(B) His many knowledge

(C) His knowledge

(D) Knowledges

② TOEIC®頻出名詞の語法とは？

One of my colleagues has decided to attend a certain ------- in Hawaii.

(A) refund

(B) extent

(C) workshop

(D) amenity

③ 注意を要する代名詞とは？

While some people save more than average, ------- borrow more than average.

(A) he

(B) others

(C) another

(D) other

Unit 11 で押さえる文法のルール

Rule 29 可算名詞と不可算名詞の違い

可算名詞	決定詞 a / an や、複数で語尾に（- e）s。個数を表す表現がつく。
不可算名詞	a / an はつかず複数語尾にならない。量を表す表現がつく。

【TOEIC でも問われる代表的な不可算名詞】

knowledge（知識）　advice（助言）　baggage[luggage]（荷物）　clothing（衣類）

Rule 30 代名詞の注意点

① 単数 / 複数 ［単数］this, that, it, one ［複数］these, those, they, ones

② 修飾語の位置 that / those は後置修飾のみ可能、one（s）は前置修飾のみ可能

③ 注意を要する代名詞用法

　　[1] 複数個からどれか1つ　⇒　one

　　[2] 別のどれか1つ　⇒　another

　　[3] 他の複数個 / 残り1つ　⇒　others / the other

Rule 31 TOEIC 頻出の名詞

	類義語で押さえる
〈お金・支払い〉	earnings（所得）　account（請求書・預金口座）　charge（料金） fare（運賃）　fee（謝礼）　cost（費用・経費）　change（小銭・釣り銭） cash（現金）　bill（請求書・紙幣）　wage（賃金）　refund（返金） incentive（奨励金）　debt（借金）　reimbursement（払い戻し） deposit（頭金）　income（収入）　allowance（手当て）
〈客〉	customer（顧客）　spectator（観客）　passenger（乗客）　client（依頼人） guest（来賓）　consumer（消費者）
〈不動産〉	property（財産）　estate agent（不動産業者）
〈株・取引・ 消費〉	stock-/shareholder（株主）　contract（契約）　distribution（分配） transaction（処理；取引）　shipping and handling charge（発送手数料） consumption tax（消費税）　invoice（送り状・請求書）　guarantee（保証） certificate（証明・保証書）　subscription（定期購読）

	場面で押さえる
〈旅行〉	participant（参加者）　departure（出発）⇔ arrival（到着）　customs（税関） itinerary（旅行日程）　aisle seat ⇔ window seat（通路⇔窓側席）
〈雇用・施設・ 工場〉	facility[amenity]（設備）　representative（代表者）　superior（上司）⇔ subordinate （部下）　equipment（装置・備品）　prototype（試作品）　employment（雇用） employer（雇用者）⇔ employee（従業員）　factory/plant（工場）　assembly line（組立ライン）　department/division/section（部門）　compliance（法令遵守）

前置詞句〈前置詞＋名詞〉で頻出の名詞
in person（直接自分で）　in stock ⇔ out of stock（在庫のある ⇔ 在庫切れの）
on display（展示して）　in place ⇔ out of place（適所に ⇔ 場違いで）　on ～ basis（～基準で）

ポイント □ルールを意識しながら問題を解く　□分からない語句にチェック　□文意の確認

1. You cannot reject ------- without giving any explanation.
   - (A) each piece of information
   - (B) lot of information
   - (C) every pieces of information
   - (D) a lot information

2. Some payments are made by -------, and others by credit card.
   - (A) charge
   - (B) cash
   - (C) fee
   - (D) fare

3. Bony and Jack are waiting for ------- to come and fix a burst water pipe.
   - (A) a retailer
   - (B) an estate agent
   - (C) a stockholder
   - (D) a plumber

4. The new leaflet on tax duty was published in ------- to taxpayer needs.
   - (A) response
   - (B) recognition
   - (C) replacement
   - (D) reference

5. Please do not hesitate to contact ------- at my mobile number if you have any queries.
   - (A) my
   - (B) mine
   - (C) myself
   - (D) me

6. The travel guidebook has long been established as a compulsory item for tourists to plan their -------.
   - (A) deposit
   - (B) prototype
   - (C) participants
   - (D) itinerary

7. Robert attends the executive meeting with his general manager on a weekly -------.
   - (A) time
   - (B) place
   - (C) basis
   - (D) stage

8. The event is open to members and ------- guests only.
   - (A) they
   - (B) her
   - (C) their
   - (D) its

9. We are sending you a free ------- to our news letter on stocks for two months.
   - (A) prescription
   - (B) reimbursement
   - (C) subscription
   - (D) invoice

10. Of the five companies, four of them use online services to a reasonable extent, while ------- makes limited use of them.
    - (A) the other
    - (B) another
    - (C) other
    - (D) the others

リスニング・セクション

PART 1 （写真描写問題）の演習 56 ~ 57

1.

Ⓐ　Ⓑ　Ⓒ　Ⓓ

2.

Ⓐ　Ⓑ　Ⓒ　Ⓓ

PART 2 （応答問題）の演習 58 ~ 60

3. Mark your answer on your answer sheet.　Ⓐ　Ⓑ　Ⓒ

4. Mark your answer on your answer sheet.　Ⓐ　Ⓑ　Ⓒ

5. Mark your answer on your answer sheet.　Ⓐ　Ⓑ　Ⓒ

Part 1 56 ～ 57

1. A: Two factory chimneys _____
    the others.
   B: Many passengers _____.
   C: _____ tracks for trains.
   D: The warehouses _____
    the architects.

2. A: The carpet _____ yet.
   B: Their luggage _____.
   C: They sit _____ own
    computer.
   D: _____ the window.

Part 2 58 ～ 60

3. _____ the agenda from _____ colleagues
   or _____?
     A: _____.
     B: You _____.
     C: _____.

4. How much is _____ house?
     A: _____.
     B: _____.
     C: _____ for the housing loan.

5. We _____ this year.
     A: _____ railing.
     B: But _____ labor cost.
     C: _____ baggage claim tag.

リーディング・セクション

PART 6（長文穴埋め問題）の演習

Questions 1-3 refer to the following article.

Blue Melody

Jazz is surely one type of American music, which ------- on a daily basis.
                                                        1.
Several clubs in New Orleans try to preserve the Blue Melody by practicing and

refining ------- every day. Many great jazz players gather weekly to give a
          2.
performance for their fans. Such performances also include soul, hip hop, R & B and

funk.

The Blue Melody has played a part in the image of New Orleans, and has also

spread to Chicago and Indiana. The Blue Melody has also become ------- in Italy,
                                                                 3.
Japan, and several other parts of the world.

Jazz has a melody that is impossible to imitate in other music genres. -------.
                                                                        4.

---

1. (A) preserves
   (B) is preserved
   (C) has preserved
   (D) preserved

2. (A) their
   (B) all
   (C) other
   (D) it

3. (A) popular
   (B) population
   (C) populace
   (D) popularity

4. (A) Therefore, there are various music genres.
   (B) Most of jazz are easy to imitate.
   (C) That's why jazz will always be around.
   (D) Instead, the Blue Melody has been spreading in a
       limited area.

Note: ☐ refine ～を洗練する

Questions 1-5 refer to the following instruction, application form, and e-mail.

HOW TO APPLY FOR SCHOLARSHIP

Apply for your favorite vocational training program from the four choices below. By clicking on the specific program you wish to apply for, you will be automatically directed to an online application form designed for the scholarship of your program. Please fill in all the blanks in the form and submit it online with some supporting documents, including two references.

Communication

Accounting

Business Strategy

Marketing

Application Form for a Scholarship in the Accounting Program

Applicant

Name: Nicholas Smith

Phone numbers: 616-555-8226 (mobile)

E-mail address: n.smith@greenlabel.com

Current Address: 335 Apple St, Holland, MI

Employment Information

Current employer: XYZ Financial Company Ltd.

Address: 1342 Apple St, Holland, MI

Gross pay: $40,000

Financial Information

Food and clothing: $5,000

Medical expenses: $2,000

Telephone and cable TV: $1,000

Vehicle payments: $5,000

Loan and credit card payments: $10,000

Date:	June 20
From:	Taylor White <t.white@scholarshipedu.com>
To:	Nicholas Smith <n.smith@greenlabel.com>

Dear Mr. Smith

Thank you for applying for a scholarship of one of our valuable vocational programs online at this time. Unfortunately, many applicants have already applied for the same program you selected. For this reason, the scholarship committee arrived at a decision that applicants will be required to have at least five years of work experience relevant to the program they wish to take. Please provide us with this information and details of why you need the scholarship.

Sincerely,

Taylor White
Scholarship Director

1. In the instruction, the word "specific" in paragraph 1, line 2, is closest in meaning to
(A) particular
(B) favorite
(C) urgent
(D) crucial

2. In the instruction, what are applicants NOT asked to submit?
(A) References
(B) An application form
(C) Supporting documents
(D) A photo

3. Which program did Mr. Smith apply for?
(A) Communication
(B) Accounting
(C) Business Strategy
(D) Marketing

4. What is most likely true about Mr. Smith's personal information?
(A) His house would be located far away from the company he is working for.
(B) He spends most on food and clothing.
(C) His take-home salary is less than $40,000.
(D) He uses a landline phone instead of a cell phone.

5. What did Taylor White ask in her e-mail?
(A) Whether Mr. Smith has any medical problems
(B) Whether Mr. Smith has appropriate work experience
(C) Whether Mr. Smith earns enough
(D) Whether Mr. Smith is able to commute to the venue of the program

Notes: ☐ vocational 職業の ☐ gross pay 給与総額

1) 以下の文を和訳しましょう（空欄には適切な代名詞を補ってください）。

❶ The scholarship committee arrived at a decision that applicants will be required to have at least five years of work experience relevant to the program they wish to take. PART 7, e-mail, *line* 3

_____

_____

(ポイント：名詞と形容詞表現)

❷ Of the five companies, four of them use online services to a reasonable extent, while (   ) makes limited use of them. PART 5, (10)

_____

(ポイント：代名詞の選択)

2) 頻出名詞を英英辞典の語義定義から選んでみよう。

❶ (   )：an agreement or arrangement, especially in business or politics, that helps both sides involved.
a) teleconference   b) subscription   c) deal   d) shipping charge

❷ (   )：a list of things provided or work done together with their cost, for payment at a later time.
a) guarantee   b) invoice   c) refund   d) contract

❸ (   )：someone who has a lower position and less authority than someone else in an organization.
a) supervisor   b) representative   c) personnel   d) subordinate

❹ (   )：a plan or list of the places you will visit on a journey.
a) participant   b) luggage claim tag   c) itinerary   d) customs

❺ (   )：available in a particular shop.
a) out of stock   b) stock market   c) in stock   d) in person

Unit 11　頻出 Words & Phrases 61

	W&P	発音	意味	Tips
☐1	**preserve**	/prɪzə́:rv/	動 ～を保護する	名 preservation 保護；保全
☐2	**warehouse**	/wéərhàus/	名 倉庫	
☐3	**agenda**	/ədʒéndə/	名 議題	
☐4	**rent**	/rent/	形 借り賃；家賃 動 ～を賃借りする	動 ～を賃借りする
☐5	**location**	/loukéɪʃ(ə)n/	名 所在地	動 locate ～の位置を定める
☐6	**budget**	/bʌ́dʒət/	名 予算	
☐7	**railing**	/réɪlɪŋ/	名 手すり	
☐8	**lower**	/lóuər/	動 ～を下げる	
☐9	**baggage claim**	/bǽɡɪdʒ klèɪm/	名 手荷物受取所	
☐10	**remodel**	/rì:má(:)d(ə)l/	動 建物を改築する	= renovate / refurbish
☐11	**appropriate**	/əpróupriət/	形 適切な；ふさわしい	
☐12	**reference**	/réf(ə)r(ə)ns/	名 推薦書、言及	句 with[in]reference to ～に関して
☐13	**valuable**	/vǽljəb(ə)l/	形 価値のある	
☐14	**committee**	/kəmíti/	名 委員会	
☐15	**urgent**	/ə́:rdʒ(ə)nt/	形 緊急の	副 urgently 緊急に
☐16	**crucial**	/krú:ʃ(ə)l/	形 重要な	= essential / critical
☐17	**venue**	/vénju:/	名 開催場所	
☐18	**payment**	/péɪmənt/	名 支払い	動 pay 払う
☐19	**leaflet**	/lí:flət/	名 ちらし；小冊子	≒ brochure
☐20	**duty**	/djú:ti/	名 義務；職務	句 on duty 勤務中の ⇔ off duty 非番で
☐21	**publish**	/pʌ́blɪʃ/	動 ～を出版する	名 publication 出版（物）
☐22	**reject**	/rɪdʒékt/	動 ～を拒絶する	= decline / turn down
☐23	**compulsory**	/kəmpʌ́ls(ə)ri/	形 必須の；義務的な	
☐24	**plumber**	/plʌ́mər/	名 配管工	★発音注意
☐25	**invoice**	/ínvɔɪs/	名 請求書	
☐26	**prescription**	/prɪskrípʃ(ə)n/	名 処方箋、処方薬	
☐27	**subscription**	/səbskrípʃ(ə)n/	名 定期購読（料/期間）	
☐28	**deposit**	/dɪpá(:)zət/	名 頭金、手付金	
☐29	**prototype**	/próutətàɪp/	名 試作品	
☐30	**itinerary**	/aɪtínərèri/	名 旅行日程	

Unit 12 副詞と重要構文

基本問題

① **TOEIC 頻出の副詞とは？**

It is ------- rare for a firm to have an absolute monopoly of the market.

    (A) closely   (B) relatively

    (C) immediately   (D) shortly

---

② **文と文とを結びつける論理接続の副詞の注意点とは？**

People buy cars infrequently, ------- rarely visit car dealers.

    (A) therefore   (B) however   (C) and therefore   (D) in conclusion

---

③ **倒置が起こる条件とは？**

------- does Jenny leave her office during office hours.

    (A) Merely   (B) Hardly   (C) What   (D) So

Unit 12 で押さえる文法のルール

Rule 32　副詞の役割

副詞：英文の要素（主語・目的語・補語）にならず、動詞・形容詞や文全体を修飾。

構造把握では除いて考えますが、否定の副詞は文意に影響するので注意。

==

【時間を表す副詞】

  [現在時] now / currently（現在は）　nowadays（この頃は）　these days（最近は）

  [現在完了時] recently（最近）　lately（最近）　latest（一番遅く）

【頻度を表す副詞】

  always（いつも）⇒ typically / generally / normally / usually（たいてい）

  ⇒ often / frequently（よく）⇒ occasionally / sometimes（時々）

  ⇒ rarely / seldom（めったに～ない）⇒ never（決して～ない）

  [annually（年1回）/ yearly / monthly / weekly（年 / 月 / 週1回）]

【否定を表す副詞】

  [動作] hardly / scarcely / barely（ほとんど～ない）[cf. hard（一生懸命）]

  [頻度] rarely / seldom

【形容詞と同形の副詞】

  late（副 遅く ⇔ 形 遅い）　latest（副 一番遅く ⇔ 形 最新の）

Rule 33 文と文とを結びつける副詞の注意点

あくまで副詞なので、接続詞・関係詞のように、節と節とを直接結合することはできません。

× People buy cars infrequently, *therefore* rarely visit car dealers.

以下の2つの方法で用います。また、各副詞はイメージでまとめて覚えましょう。

① [接続詞の追加]

People buy cars infrequently, and *therefore* rarely visit car dealers.

② [独立した文を結合]

People buy cars infrequently. *Therefore*, they rarely visit car dealers.

（人は頻繁に車を購入しません。よって、めったに自動車販売店を訪れません。）

【TOEIC 頻出　文と文とを結びつける副詞】

帰結・結果 ⇒	accordingly　　as a result　　consequently　　eventually　　hence　　therefore　　thus
追加　＋	additionally（in addition）　　besides　　furthermore　　moreover
対比・逆接 ⇔	by/in contrast　　however　　meanwhile（in the meantime）　　nevertheless　　yet
類似／要約 ＝	likewise　　similarly / in conclusion [short, summary]　　to sum up

Rule 34 倒置構文の3パターン

① 〔否定語句が文頭〕

Not only <u>did the guests</u> enjoy an excellent meal, but they were also entertained.

② 〔so, nor, neither が節の頭に来る反復表現〕

As output and sales rise, *so* <u>does total cost</u>.

These data are not objective, and *neither* <u>are they</u> reliable.

③ 〔仮定法の if 省略〕（Unit 9 **Rule 25** を参照）

ポイント □ルールを意識しながら問題を解く　□分からない語句にチェック　□文意の確認

1. Most companies tend to rely ------- on electronic records.
   - (A) exclusive
   - (B) exclusion
   - (C) exclude
   - (D) exclusively

2. What brands of cosmetics have you seen advertised -------?
   - (A) recent
   - (B) latest
   - (C) lately
   - (D) currently

3. I worked ------- at the department to be promoted to a manager.
   - (A) hardly
   - (B) finally
   - (C) seldom
   - (D) hard

4. If the survey is ------- conducted, the results are reliable.
   - (A) easily
   - (B) properly
   - (C) approvingly
   - (D) originally

5. The company expects, ------- the budget constraints, that the development of new products will be successful.
   - (A) despite
   - (B) nevertheless
   - (C) though
   - (D) even so

6. They have experienced the recession in the past ------- are better able to handle it.
   - (A) for that matter
   - (B) therefore
   - (C) and as a result
   - (D) and otherwise

7. It is neither practical to abolish the plant, ------- is it right to do so.
   - (A) nor
   - (B) while
   - (C) or
   - (D) consequently

8. You will be asked to complete an application form and ------- to attend training.
   - (A) much
   - (B) securely
   - (C) lonely
   - (D) subsequently

9. Lectures and workshops have been planned for Wednesday 4 and Thursday 5 November, -------.
   - (A) occasionally
   - (B) steadily
   - (C) fairly
   - (D) respectively

10. The service department ------- responded to the complaints from customers about the new product.
    - (A) courteously
    - (B) approximately
    - (C) slightly
    - (D) considerably

リスニング・セクション

PART 2 (応答問題)の演習　62 ~ 64

1. Mark your answer on your answer sheet.　Ⓐ　Ⓑ　Ⓒ

2. Mark your answer on your answer sheet.　Ⓐ　Ⓑ　Ⓒ

3. Mark your answer on your answer sheet.　Ⓐ　Ⓑ　Ⓒ

PART 4 (説明文問題)の演習　65

4. Who most likely are the listeners?
　(A) Mobile phone users
　(B) Only company executives
　(C) Donors
　(D) Coworkers

5. What does the man imply when he says, "After much trial and error"?
　(A) The ID chip was not hard to find in a mobile phone store.
　(B) The ID chip was difficult to develop.
　(C) He tried to make the ID chip work without any malfunction.
　(D) He spent a lot of money purchasing the ID chip.

6. What does the speaker mention about the result of the development?
　(A) The company has made a profit.
　(B) He has got a special bonus.
　(C) Other companies in the industry have been sharing the chip data.
　(D) His company has received an award.

ディクテイションにチャレンジ！

Part 2 62 ~ 64

1. _____ the promotion campaign?

    A: _____ business.

    B: _____ .

    C: The _____ .

2. _____ sometime next week?

    A: Well, _____ ?

    B: _____ .

    C: The _____ .

3. What was the client's _____ ?

    A: The client _____ .

    B: _____ .

    C: _____ .

シャドウイング＆オーバーラッピングにチャレンジ！

Part 4 65

★ 「連結」「脱落」「同化」など音声変化に気を付けながら、音声を聞き、まずは後について発音してみましょう。次に、音声と同じスピードで発音してみましょう。発音と一緒に意味もとりながら挑戦してみましょう。

Well, firs(t)ly I woul(d) like to thank the executive team for choosing me as "employee of the year." I've spent_all my time developing_an ID chi(p) tha(t) can be integrated into a mobile phone. After much trial and_error, a mobile phone wi(th) the ID chip is now on the market. It_allows users to drive_a car an(d) withdraw money from a bank account withou(t) any other form of ID. Since the release, inquiries_abou(t) the chip_an(d) new contracts for it have been increasing. This_is_all_I wanted, an(d) so receiving this award is_a pure bonus. An(d) finally, many people who have helped_an(d) supporte(d) me in whatever I have been involved_in share this awar(d) with me, especially my family. Thank you all.

リーディング・セクション

PART 6 (長文穴埋め問題)の演習

Questions 1-4 refer to the following information.

The Mid River Community Center

The Mid River Community Center is a locally-run organization adjacent to the City Hall. The organization was established 15 years ago. It aims to serve people who moved to the United States from other countries. -------, ten volunteers and over 30
1.
students take advantage of the programs available. The center offers after-school homework help for junior high and high school students. It also has volunteer-taught English language classes for adults. ------- of these services are free. In addition, the
2.
Mid River Community Center hosts a variety of social events throughout the year.
-------. People who are resident in the community are ------- to come to the Mid River
3.   **4.**
Community Center to enjoy local dishes and traditional music.

For further details, visit our Web site at www.mid-river-community.org, or contact us by phone at 198-555-1000.

---

1. (A) Still
(B) Currently
(C) Previously
(D) Consequently

2. (A) Both
(B) Almost
(C) Each
(D) Every

3. (A) The most popular event is the annual Autumn Festival.
(B) These are offered to the best performers.
(C) Event organizers do not recommend attending.
(D) Private consultations are available by request.

4. (A) invite
(B) invites
(C) inviting
(D) invited

Note: □ adjacent to ～に隣接した

Questions 1–5 refer to the following memo, Web page, and e-mail.

MEMO

From: Irma Velasquez, Personnel Manager

To: All staff

Date: March 5

As announced last year, Gorman Consulting's office in São Paolo, Brazil, will begin operation in September. Most positions will be filled by employees recruited locally. However, there are some exciting opportunities available for personnel at other Gorman Consulting offices around the world.

To be considered for a position, visit the Careers section of our internal Web site and submit your résumé by the stated deadline. For all listed openings, the company will cover moving expenses, assist with the relocation process (including visas and other paperwork), and provide Portuguese language lessons prior to departure.

---

https://www.gormanconsulting.com/careers/brazil/civilengineeringdesigner

---

Title: Civil Engineering Designer

An experienced civil engineering designer is needed for our new office in São Paolo. The successful candidate will work closely with local personnel to deliver engineering consulting services to public and private clients in Brazil. Duties include: producing designs, plans, and drawings; coordinating and preparing estimates, bids, and contracts; and ensuring compliance with timelines, budgets, and quality standards.

Criteria: The position requires a degree in civil engineering and at least five years' experience within Gorman Consulting. Strong communication skills are essential. Applicants must also have expertise with using drafting software and quality management systems. Preference will be given to highly motivated team players who demonstrate initiative and leadership.

Deadline: March 30. To apply, click here.

To:	Michael Kula <m.kula@gormanconsulting.com>
From:	Irma Velazquez <i.velazquez@gormanconsulting.com>
Date:	May 5
Re:	Civil Engineering Designer position

Hi Michael,

Congratulations once again on being selected for this exciting new role. I am sure working in São Paolo will be a great professional and personal experience for you.

We will begin making preparations for your transfer soon. The main priority is to get the visa process under way quickly, so that everything will be in place before you leave on September 3. We will be sending you the necessary paperwork once it is ready.

In the coming weeks, we will also be in touch regarding moving arrangements and other preparations. In the meantime, I have attached a helpful pamphlet with general information and advice about international transfers. If you ever have any questions, please feel free to contact me.

Irma Velazquez
Personnel Manager

1. What does Ms. Velasquez indicate about the São Paolo office?
   (A) It was established last year.
   (B) It will help create new jobs in other countries.
   (C) It will mainly seek employees in Brazil.
   (D) It has almost finished recruiting staff.

2. What is NOT one of the civil engineering designer's duties?
   (A) Providing consulting services to customers
   (B) Preparing legal documents
   (C) Making sure projects finish on time
   (D) Training local personnel

3. What qualification does Mr. Kula probably possess?
   (A) A design degree
   (B) Software development skills
   (C) Management experience
   (D) Leadership ability

4. What is the purpose of the e-mail?
   (A) To advise a colleague to apply for a job
   (B) To describe the next steps in a process
   (C) To verify that some paperwork is complete
   (D) To welcome a recently transferred employee

5. What will Mr. Kula most likely do before September 3?

(A) Take Portuguese lessons
(B) Obtain a professional qualification
(C) Visit the São Paolo office
(D) Move into a new residence

精読コーナー

1) 和訳しましょう。

❶ People who are resident in the community are invited to come to the Community Center to enjoy local dishes and traditional music. PART 6, *line* 8

_____

ポイント：関係詞と不定詞

❷ I am sure working in São Paolo will be a great professional and personal experience for you. PART 7, *line* 1

_____

ポイント：接続詞thatの省略と動名詞 ★ S ＋ **思考・発言のV** (that) S' ＋ V' ... .
that は省略されることがあるので、補って構文を把握します。

❸ He does not want to boss the firm, nor does he want to send in a manager. PART 5, (7)

_____

ポイント：否定表現による倒置 □ boss 〜を牛耳る

2) (　　　) に適する語を選択肢から選びなさい。

❶ Gorman Consulting's office in Paris will begin operation in September. Most positions will be filled by employees recruited locally. (　　　), there are some exciting opportunities available for personnel at other Gorman Consulting offices around the world.

a) Therefore　　b) In addition to　　c) However　　d) Likewise

❷ The present system is the most profitable (　　　) it is strongly suggested that no changes are implemented.

a) furthermore　　b) therefore　　c) but in contrast　　d) and therefore

❸ The Japanese term "hai" is literally translated as "yes", although it can also mean "I see" and does not necessarily mean agreement. (　　　), the Japanese are reluctant to give a direct "no" answer, because they emphasize harmony rather than confrontation.

a) Furthermore　　b) However　　c) For example　　d) In conclusion

□ confrontation 対立

Unit 12　頻出 Words & Phrases 66

	W&P	発音	意味	Tips
☐1	**aim to V**		㋕ ～するよう努力する	
☐2	**serve**	/sə́:rv/	㋟ ～するために尽くす ㋓ service 奉仕	
☐3	**host**	/houst/	㋟ ～を主催する	
☐4	**resident**	/rézɪd(ə)nt/	㋲ 住人 ㋟ 住んでいる	★ residence 住居
☐5	**constraint**	/kənstréɪnt/	㋲ 制限；制約	＝ restriction
☐6	**operation**	/à(:)pəréɪʃ(ə)n/	㋲ 仕事；運転	㋕ in ～ 運転中／経営中で
☐7	**lecture**	/léktʃər/	㋲ 講義	
☐8	**relocation**	/ri:loukéɪʃ(ə)n/	㋲ 移転	㋟ relocate 移転する／させる
☐9	**prior to**		㋕ ～の前に	＝ before
☐10	**experienced**	/ɪkspíəriənst/	㋟ 経験豊かな	
☐11	**estimate**	/éstɪmèɪt/	㋟ 見積もる ㋲ 見積もり	
☐12	**ensure**	/ɪnʃúər/	㋟ ～を確実にする	
☐13	**adjacent to**		㋕ ～に隣接した	
☐14	**proposal**	/prəpóuz(ə)l/	㋲ 提案 ★語尾注意	㋟ propose (＋that SV) 　～を提案する
☐15	**reply**	/rɪpláɪ/	㋟ 返事をする ㋲ 返事	
☐16	**withdraw**	/wɪðdrɔ́:/	㋟ ～を引き出す	
☐17	**bid**	/bɪd/	㋲ 入札 ㋟ 入札する	㋲ bidder 入札者
☐18	**inquiry**	/ínkwəri/	㋲ 問い合わせ	
☐19	**award**	/əwɔ́:rd/	㋲ 賞 ㋟ 与える	
☐20	**especially**	/ɪspéʃ(ə)li/	㋐ 特に；特別に	
☐21	**securely**	/sɪkjúərli/	㋐ 安全に；しっかり	㋟ secure 安定した；安全な ㋲ security 安全
☐22	**profit**	/prá(:)fət/	㋲ 利益 ㋟ ～から利益を得る (＋ from)	
☐23	**exclusively**	/ɪksklú:sɪvli/	㋐ もっぱら	㋟ exclusive
☐24	**conduct**	/kəndʌ́kt/ /ká(:)ndʌkt/	㋟ ～を行う ㋲ 行動	
☐25	**properly**	/prá(:)pərli/	㋐ 適切に	㋟ proper 適切な
☐26	**originally**	/ərídʒ(ə)n(ə)li/	㋐ 元々	㋟ original 元の
☐27	**subsequently**	/sʌ́bsɪkw(ə)ntli/	㋐ その後	㋟ subsequent その後の
☐28	**departure**	/dɪpá:rtʃər/	㋲ 出発	⇔ arrival 到着
☐29	**personnel**	/pə̀:rsənél/	㋲ 職員 ㋟ 人事の	㋕ personnel department 人事課
☐30	**malfunction**	/mælfʌ́ŋ(k)ʃ(ə)n/	㋲ 不具合；故障	

Unit 13 模擬問題

Part 1

1.

Ⓐ Ⓑ Ⓒ Ⓓ

2.

Ⓐ Ⓑ Ⓒ Ⓓ

Part 2

3. Mark your answer on your answer sheet.　　Ⓐ Ⓑ Ⓒ

4. Mark your answer on your answer sheet.　　Ⓐ Ⓑ Ⓒ

5. Mark your answer on your answer sheet.　　Ⓐ Ⓑ Ⓒ

6. Mark your answer on your answer sheet.　　Ⓐ Ⓑ Ⓒ

7. Mark your answer on your answer sheet.　　Ⓐ Ⓑ Ⓒ

8. Mark your answer on your answer sheet. Ⓐ Ⓑ Ⓒ

9. Mark your answer on your answer sheet. Ⓐ Ⓑ Ⓒ

10. Mark your answer on your answer sheet. Ⓐ Ⓑ Ⓒ

11. What is the purpose of the woman's call?
  (A) To request more work
  (B) To give a recommendation
  (C) To discuss research results
  (D) To ask for revisions

12. What did the man do?
  (A) Designed a Web page
  (B) Interviewed job applicants
  (C) Requested a higher rate
  (D) Wrote an executive profile

13. What does the woman tell the man?
  (A) She is not in a hurry to begin.
  (B) She needs him to start tomorrow.
  (C) She will pay him next month.
  (D) She has to verify her availability.

14. Where do the speakers most likely work?
  (A) At a school
  (B) At a convention center
  (C) At a travel agency
  (D) At a hotel

15. What is indicated about the trip to Dover?
  (A) It has become popular.
  (B) It is very long.
  (C) It is inexpensive.
  (D) It will start soon.

16. What is the woman's main concern?
  (A) Arranging hotel rooms
  (B) Finding more participants
  (C) Increasing the budget
  (D) Organizing transportation

17. What does the speakers' company plan to do?
    (A) Make an announcement to the media
    (B) Change its business hours
    (C) Merge with another company
    (D) Open a new branch office

18. What does the woman mean when she says, "I'm about to wrap up here"?
    (A) She will send a document shortly.
    (B) She is having trouble with a project.
    (C) She will soon go home.
    (D) She is finishing a meeting.

19. What will the woman do within the next hour?
    (A) Install some software
    (B) Check a document
    (C) Finalize a translation
    (D) Contact the Seoul office

Time	Topic
9:30 A.M.	Office safety procedures
10:00 A.M.	Workers union membership drive
10:30 A.M.	Health benefits for employees
11:00 A.M.	Mentoring program orientation

20. What do the speakers say Abbie Wu will do?
    (A) Move to another office
    (B) Organize an orientation
    (C) Give a presentation
    (D) Take part in safety training

21. Why is the man concerned?
    (A) He will not be able to meet Abbie Wu.
    (B) He has a lot of information to discuss.
    (C) He is missing some materials.
    (D) He does not have time to read a document.

22. Look at the graphic. When will the man most likely give his talk?
    (A) 9:30 A.M.
    (B) 10:00 A.M.
    (C) 10:30 A.M.
    (D) 11:00 A.M.

Part 4 🎧 **73**

23. Who is the speaker?
(A) A university professor
(B) A computer technician
(C) A radio host
(D) An office manager

24. What was the study mainly about?
(A) The falling cost of computer technology
(B) The relationship between computers and work
(C) The decreasing size of digital devices
(D) Recent causes of unemployment

25. What will Dr. Hayden give advice about?
(A) Ways to work more productively
(B) Tips for repairing computers
(C) Finding jobs in the technology sector
(D) Purchasing digital devices cheaply

🎧 **74**

26. What is the purpose of the call?
(A) To announce a location change
(B) To provide an update
(C) To recommend a candidate
(D) To request a reservation

27. What does the speaker imply when he says, "it wouldn't be the first time"?
(A) He has already worked with MRZ Associates.
(B) He has visited a location before.
(C) He may have made a mistake.
(D) He might be late for an appointment.

28. According to the message, what will Rina Takemoto do for Brian?
(A) Interview him for a position
(B) Meet him at a nearby station
(C) Show him to a conference room
(D) Send him a list of employees

Crane	Gull		Ibis
West			East
Plover	Heron		

29. What problem does the speaker indicate about the Plover Room?
(A) The projector did not work.
(B) It was too small.
(C) There was too much noise.
(D) It was too bright.

30. What does the speaker ask Marla to do?
(A) Replace some presentation equipment
(B) Go to the meeting room 10 minutes early
(C) Wait for the board members in the lobby
(D) Contact the meeting participants

31. Look at the graphic. Where will the speaker give his presentation tomorrow?
(A) The Heron Room
(B) The Ibis Room
(C) The Gull Room
(D) The Crane Room

Part 5 目標タイム：1問 25 秒～30 秒→設問 32～41 を 5 分以内！
Your time: _____

32. When the economy is weak, consumers tend to avoid making large purchases due to ------- concerns.
(A) financed
(B) finances
(C) financial
(D) financially

33. Use the fire escape at the end of the hall to exit the building ------- fire or other emergency.
(A) in case of
(B) as opposed to
(C) in relation to
(D) by means of

34. The auto industry posted good results last quarter, as sales of new vehicles ------- analysts' projections.
(A) advised
(B) oversaw
(C) exceeded
(D) impressed

35. Dimitra Pullen ------- by Mitford Tires' board of directors to take over for retiring CEO Hugh Chelin.
(A) appoint
(B) appointed
(C) was appointing
(D) was appointed

36. Passwords that use a combination of letters and numbers are ------- more secure than those with only letters.
(A) far   (B) very
(C) either   (D) such

37. The manager's responsibilities include ensuring that sales assistants perform their tasks -------.
(A) possibly
(B) wholly
(C) rightfully
(D) efficiently

38. Nelda Cesar's success as superintendent of Washington's largest school district is ------- the way the country thinks about education.
(A) change
(B) changing
(C) changed
(D) changes

39. Unless they are unplugged, many appliances and electronic devices will consume electrical power ------- when they are turned off.
(A) despite   (B) during
(C) even   (D) throughout

40. Residents of Kalimba will be able to travel easily between downtown and the airport ------- the new Metroline subway begins operation next year.
(A) although   (B) upon
(C) including   (D) once

41. Strict limits have been placed on water usage in Calavera County ------- a two-month period with almost no rainfall.
(A) following   (B) follow
(C) followed   (D) followers

Questions 42-45 refer to the following information.

-------- .
42.

If you are expecting a guest, use the Cortix reservation system to make sure that your visitor is able to access the building. If ------- , the reception desk will be informed
43.
of your visitor's expected arrival time.

Please be aware that access to the building will be allowed up to 10 minutes before and 30 minutes after this time. Contact the security office if you need to make a change to any -------.
44.

Guests will be issued a badge which ------- them to pass through the automated
45.
security gate.

Visitors must keep this badge on them at all times while on the premises. To exit, visitors insert the badge into the slot next to the security gate.

42. (A) The reception desk will be closed tomorrow.
(B) Thank you for visiting our company.
(C) Your membership is about to expire.
(D) All visits to this facility must be pre-authorized.

43. (A) approve
(B) approved
(C) approval
(D) approvingly

44. (A) reason
(B) entry
(C) deadline
(D) appointment

45. (A) permits
(B) is permitted
(C) is permitting
(D) permitting

Part 7

目標タイム：設問 46〜47 を 2 分以内！
Your time: _____

Questions 46-47 refer to the following text message chain.

Hamish Currie [1:35 P.M.]	Hi Morag. I'm at the doctor's office for a checkup. My appointment was for 1:00, but I'm still waiting to see him.
Morag Baird [1:36 P.M.]	Don't you have to be back here for a meeting with Highland Development at 2:30?
Hamish Currie [1:37 P.M.]	I do indeed. But it's not looking good. Could you take my place?
Morag Baird [1:38 P.M.]	I don't know much about the project.
Hamish Currie [1:40 P.M.]	Talk to Angus. He can give you the agenda and fill you in on the key points.
Morag Baird [1:41 P.M.]	OK, then. I'll do that now.
Hamish Currie [1:42 P.M.]	Angus will lead the meeting, so you won't need to say much. He just wants someone from the IT department there in case the client has any technical questions.
Morag Baird [1:43 P.M.]	OK, I'll do my best. Don't worry.

46. At 1:37 P.M., what does Mr. Currie mean when he says, "It's not looking good"?
   (A) He has not finished preparing.
   (B) He is not feeling well.
   (C) He is likely to miss a meeting.
   (D) He thinks the client is unhappy.

47. What will Ms. Baird most likely do next?
   (A) Talk to the IT department about a problem
   (B) Attend a meeting at a client's office
   (C) Forward an agenda to a colleague
   (D) Discuss a project with Angus

Questions 48-51 refer to the following article.

Sydney, NSW (August 30)—After 120 years of operation, an Australian institution is expanding overseas next year. Redmond, the country's largest department store chain, will open its first international branches in several Asian countries. It currently has 52 locations across Australia.

"Asia is the perfect match for Redmond," said CEO Oliver Fisher. "Our brand, especially our flagship Sydney branch, is very popular with tourists from Japan, South Korea, and elsewhere. The Asian market has many discerning consumers willing to pay extra for premium products and exclusive quality.   —[1]—. That's exactly what we offer."

The first overseas branch will open in Tokyo next March, with others to follow later in Seoul, Shanghai, and Singapore. —[2]—. According to Fisher, the Asian stores will feature many of the same products sold at Australian branches. However, they will also tailor their selections to suit local tastes.

—[3]—. Fisher was appointed three years ago thanks to his record of achieving rapid growth at other retailers. Since then, the company has bought out struggling rival Menzies, rebranding ten of its locations as Redmond stores. —[4]—. This is the same market it will be aiming to reach in Asia.

48. What is NOT true of Redmond?
   (A) It was founded over a century ago.
   (B) It sells high-quality merchandise.
   (C) It was purchased by a Japanese company.
   (D) It is appreciated by Asian consumers.

49. What is indicated about Redmond's Asian branches?
   (A) They will cater mainly to Australian tourists.
   (B) They will all open by the end of March.
   (C) They will occupy former Menzies locations.
   (D) They will have different product lineups.

50. According to the article, why was Oliver Fisher chosen as Redmond's CEO?
   (A) He obtained fast results at other companies.
   (B) He has managed various international chains.
   (C) He set new sales records at the flagship store.
   (D) He is an expert in the Asian retail market.

51. In which of the positions marked [1], [2], [3], and [4] does the following sentence best belong?
   "It has also shifted its advertising to focus on younger consumers."
   (A) [1]
   (B) [2]
   (C) [3]
   (D) [4]

124

目標タイム：設問 52～56 を 6 分以内！
Your time: _____

Questions 52–56 refer to the following notice and e-mails.

The Orville Chamber of Commerce presents
A One-Day Workshop with Laura Kilbey
January 27, 9 A.M. – 3:30 P.M.

Dr. Kilbey, a professor of business administration at Proctor College and the author of the bestselling *Hard Bargains*, published her second book *Deal-Makers and Deal-Breakers* earlier this month. Her intensive workshop is divided into four parts:

· 9 A.M. – 10:25 A.M.: Cultivating Your Own Style – Drive a hard bargain or take a laid back approach? This session helps you refine your personal style.

· 10:35 A.M. – 12:05 P.M.: Knowing When to Compromise – Learn to set priorities and decide where you're willing to compromise and where you're not flexible.

· 12:35 – 1:55 P.M.: Managing Your Emotions – This session provides tips on maintaining good relations.

· 2:05 – 3:30 P.M.: When to Walk Away – Be prepared to say no. This session tells you how to know when a deal just isn't possible.

Registration is $40. E-mail registration@orvillechamber.org to sign up.

To:	Laura Kilbey
From:	Vikram Chowdry
Date:	February 2
Subject:	Workshop Request

Dear Ms. Kilbey,

I attended your workshop last week and thought many of your observations would be relevant to the members of my telemarketing personnel here at DFW Solutions. In particular, I thought the lessons of the opening session would be highly valuable in their daily work and careers. Would you be interested in leading a short workshop on that topic? If so, please contact me at 417-555-3191.

I look forward to your response.

Vikram Chowdry
Sales Manager

To:	Telemarketing Team Staff
From:	Vikram Chowdry
Date:	February 12
Re:	Workshop on February 28

Dear all,

Author Laura Kilbey will lead a workshop here on February 28, from 9:00 to 10:30 A.M. in the large conference room. All team members are expected to take part. If you cannot make it, you should fill out an absence consent form for me to sign in advance.

Ms. Kilbey is an engaging instructor with many practical insights. As a preview, I have attached a passage from her new book which I found especially helpful. Please read it when you have a moment.

Vikram Chowdry
Sales Manager

52. What was the main topic of the January 27 workshop?
(A) Career development
(B) Telephone sales
(C) Management skills
(D) Negotiating techniques

53. In the first e-mail, the word "observations" in paragraph 1, line 1, is closest in meaning to
(A) measurements
(B) remarks
(C) evaluations
(D) studies

54. What subject does Mr. Chowdry want Ms. Kilbey to address at his company?
(A) Bargaining for a lower price
(B) Setting priorities at work
(C) Developing a personal style
(D) Building friendly relationships

55. Where will Ms. Kilbey speak on February 28?
(A) At the office of DFW Solutions
(B) At the Orville Chamber of Commerce
(C) At Proctor College
(D) At a telemarketing conference

56. What did Mr. Chowdry send to his team members?
(A) A form for signing up for an activity
(B) A detailed workshop agenda
(C) An article from a business magazine
(D) An excerpt from *Deal-Makers and Deal-Breakers*

		W&P	発音	意味	Tips
☐	1	appliance	/əplá(ɪ)əns/	名 器具；電化製品	
☐	2	avoid	/əvɔ́ɪd/	動 ～を避ける	句 avoid Ving V することを避ける
☐	3	at all times		句 いつでも	句 = always
☐	4	greet	/griːt/	動 人を迎える	名 greeting 挨拶
☐	5	candidate	/kǽndɪdèɪt/	名 候補者；志願者	★語尾注意
☐	6	reception	/rɪsépʃ(ə)n/	名 受付	名 receptionist 受付係
☐	7	verify	/vérɪfàɪ/	動 ～を確かめる	名 verification 確認；照合
☐	8	intensive	/ɪnténsɪv/	形 集中的な；徹底的な	
☐	9	refine	/rɪfáɪn/	動 ～を洗練・改良する	
☐	10	flexible	/fléksəb(ə)l/	形 柔軟な；融通の利く	= adaptable
☐	11	discerning	/dɪsə́ːrnɪŋ, -zə́ːrnɪŋ/	形 見識のある	動 discern ～を理解する；認める
☐	12	escort	/ɪskɔ́ːrt/	動 人を案内する	
☐	13	productivity	/pròudʌktívəti/	名 生産性	形 productive 生産力のある
☐	14	organize	/ɔ́ːrgənàɪz/	動 ～を準備/組織する	名 organization 団体；組織
☐	15	hire	/haɪər/	動 ～を雇う	≒ employ
☐	16	compromise	/kά(ː)mprəmàɪz/	動 妥協する 名 妥協	
☐	17	relevant to		句 ～に関連した	
☐	18	consent	/kənsént/	名 動 同意（する）	
☐	19	engaging	/ɪngéɪdʒɪŋ/	形 魅力的な	名 engagement 約束
☐	20	unplug	/ənplʌ́g/	動 〈コンセントなどを〉抜く	
☐	21	obtain	/əbtéɪn/	動 ～を獲得する	
☐	22	merchandise	/mə́ːrtʃ(ə)ndàɪz/	名 商品	動 ～を取引する
☐	23	appreciate	/əpríːʃièɪt/	動 ～を認める	句 I appreciate it. 感謝します
☐	24	tailor	/téɪlər/	動 ～を調整する	
☐	25	corridor	/kɔ́ːrədər/	名 通路	
☐	26	cater to		句 ～に応じる	名 catering 出前
☐	27	in case		句 万が一に備えて	
☐	28	exit	/égzət, éksət/	動 ～を終了する 名 出口；退場	
☐	29	forward	/fɔ́ːrwərd/	動 ～を転送する	句 look forward to Ving/名 V/名を楽しみにする
☐	30	issue	/íʃuː/	名 問題；出版物 動 発行する	

	W&P	発音	意味	Tips
□1	contact	/ká(:)ntækt/	動 ～と連絡をとる 名 連絡；接触	
□2	take place		句 ～が開催される	
□3	intend	/ɪnténd/	動 ～を意図する；～ するつもりである (+ to V)	
□4	probab<u>ly</u>	/prá(:)bəbli/	副 おそらく；十中八 九	
□5	suggest	/səgdʒést/	動 ～を提案する；述 べる	
□6	branch	/bræn(t)ʃ/	名 支店	
□7	true	/truː/	形 当てはまる；本当 の	
□8	encourage	/ɪnkə́ːrɪdʒ/	動 人を励ます	
□9	indi<u>ca</u>te	/índɪkèɪt/	動 ～を示す；知らせ る	
□10	remind	/rimáɪnd/	動 人に（～を）思い 出させる・気づか せる（+ of）	名 reminder 通知；注意
□11	purpose	/pə́ːrpəs/	名 目的	
□12	conver<u>sa</u>tion	/kà(:)nvərséɪʃ(ə)n/	名 会話	
□13	grap<u>hic</u>	/grǽfɪk/	名 図表	
□14	following	/fá(:)louɪŋ/	形 次の	
□15	paragraph	/pǽrəgræf/	名 段落	
□16	be able to V		句 V できる	⇔ 句 be unable to V V できない
□17	in response to		句 ～に応じて；応え て	
□18	notice	/nóutəs/	名 お知らせ 動 ～に気付く	
□19	mar<u>ked</u>	/mɑːrkt/	形 印のついた	
□20	worried	/wə́ːrid/	形 不安で；心配して	句 be worried about 心配している
□21	belong	/bɪlɔ́ːŋ /	動 相応しい；（～に） 属する（+ to）	
□22	unavail<u>able</u>	/ʌ̀nəvéɪləb(ə)l/	形 入手できない；都 合がつかない	⇔ available 利用・入手できる； 出席できる
□23	subject	/sʌ́bdʒekt/	名 主題	句 be subject to … …を前提とし て
□24	recommend	/rèkəménd/	動 ～を薦める	名 recommendation 推薦 recommend Ving V することを 薦める
□25	mean	/miːn/	動 ～を意味する	

□	26	happen	/hǽp(ə)n/	動 起こる；生じる	= occur / take place
□	27	most likely		☐ 最も〜そうな	
□	28	ready	/rédi/	形 用意ができた	☐ be ready for/to V V する準備ができている
□	29	according to		☐ 〜に従って	
□	30	advertise<u>ment</u>	/ædvərtáizmənt/	名 広告	動 advertise 〜を広告する
□	31	mention	/ménʃ(ə)n/	動 〜に言及する	= refer to
□	32	invite	/inváit/	動 人を招待する	名 invit<u>ation</u> 招待（状）
□	33	imply	/impláɪ/	動 ほのめかす	名 impl<u>ication</u> 暗示
□	34	main	/mein/	形 主要な	
□	35	concern	/kənsə́:rn/	名 心配；懸念	
□	36	request	/rikwést/	名 動 （〜を）要請/依頼（する）	
□	37	discuss	/diskʌ́s/	動 〜について議論する	
□	38	ask about[for]		☐ 〜について聞く[〜を求める；請求する]	
□	39	instruct	/instrʌ́kt/	動 〜に指示する；命じる（人 to V）	名 instr<u>uction</u> 取扱説明書；指示
□	40	statement	/stéitmənt/	名 結果	
□	41	article	/á:rtɪk(ə)l/	名 記事	
□	42	survey	/sə́:vei, sərvéi/	名 動 調査（する）	
□	43	excerpt	/éksə:rpt/	名 抜粋	
□	44	although	/ɔ:lðóu/	接 〜だが	= though
□	45	form	/fɔ:rm/	名 （申込）用紙	☐ fill out/in form 用紙に記入する
□	46	tell	/tel/	動 〜を伝える	☐ tell 人 to V 人に V するように命じる
□	47	message chain		☐ メッセージのやり取り	
□	48	ask to V		☐ V したいと頼む	
□	49	policy	/pá(:)ləsi/	名 政策；方針	
□	50	receipt	/risí:t/	名 レシート	
□	51	résumé	/rézəmèi, rézjumèi/	名 履歴書	
□	52	broadcast	/brɔ́:dkæst/	名 放送	
□	53	sess<u>ion</u>	/séʃ(ə)n/	名 会合；会議	
□	54	lineup	/láinʌ̀p/	名 構成；顔ぶれ	
□	55	procedure	/prəsí:dʒər/	名 手順；やり方	
□	56	workshop	/wə́:rkʃà(:)p/	名 作業場；講習会	

☐ 57	**membership**	/mémbərʃɪp/	名 会員（権）	★ -ship「〜関係」を作る sponsorship 後援
☐ 58	**signature**	/síɡnətʃər/	名 署名；サイン	
☐ 59	**item**	/áɪtəm/	名 商品；項目	
☐ 60	**document**	/dá(:)kjəmənt/	名 書類	

リスニングの点数を伸ばす聞き取りのポイント

　英語が苦手な学習者から、英文が何を言っているか全くわからないという声をよく聞きます。しかし、実際に、音声を書き出したスクリプトを見せると、ほとんどの単語を知っているのです。では、なぜ聞き取りができないのでしょうか。それには、以下の2つの理由があります。

　　1）　単語自体を知らない
　　2）　ネイティブの発する音と自分が覚えている音がずれている

　1) は、聞き取れなくて当然ですが、多くの場合は 2) が原因です。単語自体の音がズレている場合はもちろんですが、単語と単語がつながった際に、英語特有の変化が起こり、知っているはずの語句なのに聞き取れないということがよくあります。以下はその代表的な音変化です。

【 代表的な音声変化 】　①連結　　　②脱落　　　③同化

①連結【本書では _ の印】：母音で始まる語が、直前の子音とつながって聞こえる。
　例えば、lamp の "p" と is の "i" がつながって、"pi" と聞こえます。特に、母音 (「ア、イ、ウ、エ、オ」の音) で始まる語と前の語の最後の音をつなぎ発音される傾向にあります。
　　1. The **lamp_is_**on the bed.（太字部分の聞こえ方：ランピィゾォン？！）
　　2. The lamp is in the **corner_of** the room.（コーナロヴ？！）

②脱落【本書では (カッコ) の印】：連続して発音しにくい音が、聞こえなくなる。
　連続して発音しにくい音が隣り合うとき、聞こえなくなる音が出てきます。特に、/p/, /t/, /k/, /b/, /d/, /g/ のような閉鎖音は聞こえにくくなる傾向にあります。
　　3. **Wha(t) kind_of** movie was_it?（ワッカインドブ？！）
　　4. We **wen(t) to** see a movie.（ウェントゥ？！）
　　5. **I(t) was_a** comedy.（イッワザ？！）

③同化【本書では ▨ の印】：2 つの音が混ざりあって、別の音に聞こえる。
　隣り合う音の一方が他方に、またお互い影響を及ぼすと、別の音のように聞こえる現象があります。6 の "wanna" は元々 "want to" というフレーズで、/n/ の音の直後に /t/ を発音することになりますが、/n//t/ は調音する舌の位置が同じで、/n/ を発音するために舌先を上の歯の裏側につけたまま /t/ の音を破裂させず次の音に移るため、2 つの音が混じり合います。
　　6. We jus(t) **wanna** know if we can stay here one more night.（ワナ？！）
他に、"Could you"（クジュ）、"last year"（ラスティア）などの音も "同化" にあたります。

Words & Phrases リスト

各Unit末の「頻出Words & Phrases」ならびに pp.129-131の「基本Words & Phrases 60」で取り上げている語彙リストです。

A

accept	Unit 5
accommodation	Unit 3
according to	基本60 (p.130)
account for	Unit 4
accounting	Unit 4
achieve	Unit 7
additional	Unit 4
address	Unit 10
adjacent to	Unit 12
adjustable	Unit 7
administration	Unit 10
admit	Unit 5
advertisement	基本60 (p.130)
advise	Unit 9
affordable	Unit 3
agency	Unit 9
agenda	Unit 11
agree	Unit 5
aim to V	Unit 12
allow	Unit 6
along with	Unit 7
alternative	Unit 7
although	基本60 (p.130)
announce	Unit 4
annual	Unit 3
appear	Unit 1
appliance	Unit 13
applicant	Unit 1
application	Unit 4
appoint	Unit 4
appointment	Unit 10
appreciate	Unit 13
appropriate	Unit 11
approval	Unit 3
architect	Unit 9
arrangement	Unit 3
article	基本60 (p.130)
ask about[for]	基本60 (p.130)
ask to V	基本60 (p.130)
assign	Unit 3
assignment	Unit 2
assistance	Unit 8

at all times	Unit 13
at least	Unit 10
attach	Unit 9
attend	Unit 3
attention	Unit 2
audit	Unit 5
auditorium	Unit 7
automatic	Unit 7
availability	Unit10
availabile	Unit 1
avoid	Unit 13
award	Unit 12

B

baggage claim	Unit 11
banquet	Unit 10
-based	Unit 2
be able to V	基本60 (p.129)
be aware of	Unit 9
be subject to	Unit 6
beg	Unit 3
behind schedule	Unit 8
belong	基本60 (p.129)
belongings	Unit 9
benefit	Unit 7
bid	Unit 12
board	Unit 7
booklet	Unit 5
branch	基本60 (p.129)
broadcast	基本60 (p.130)
budget	Unit 11
bureau	Unit 6
by means of	Unit 7

C

cancellation	Unit 4
candidate	Unit 13
capable	Unit 10
carry out	Unit 4
cash register	Unit 6
cater to	Unit 13
charge	Unit 6
check in	Unit 1

check-up	Unit 10
collaboration	Unit 8
commemorate	Unit 10
committee	Unit 11
compare	Unit 8
competent	Unit 4
complaint	Unit 10
complete	Unit 7
comprehensive	Unit 3
compromise	Unit 13
compulsory	Unit 11
concern	基本60 (p.130)
conclusion	Unit 9
conduct	Unit 12
conference	Unit 4
confident	Unit 2
confidentiality	Unit 2
confirm	Unit 6
conflict	Unit 3
consent	Unit 13
consider	Unit 5
considerably	Unit 2
consistent	Unit 10
constraint	Unit 12
consumer	Unit 9
contact	基本60 (p.129)
content	Unit 8
contract	Unit 4
conversation	基本60 (p.129)
convert	Unit 8
copy	Unit 1
corridor	Unit 13
coworker	Unit 5
craft	Unit 10
crate	Unit 4
crucial	Unit 11
cupboard	Unit 3
current	Unit 9
customer	Unit 2

D

deadline	Unit 6
deal with	Unit 5

監修者・編著者・著者

花田徹也（はなだ　てつや）

土屋知洋（つちや　ともひろ）

中田達也（なかた　たつや）

中川右也（なかがわ　ゆうや）

中西のりこ（なかにし　のりこ）

仁科恭徳（にしな　やすのり）

TOEIC® L&R TEST のための基礎演習

―――――――――――――――――――――――――

2020 年 2 月 20 日　　第 1 版発行

2022 年 2 月 20 日　　第 5 版発行

監修者――花田徹也

編著者――土屋知洋／中田達也

著　者――中川右也／中西のりこ／仁科恭徳

発行者――前田俊秀

発行所――株式会社 三修社

〒 150-0001 東京都渋谷区神宮前 2-2-22

TEL 03-3405-4511　　FAX 03-3405-4522

振替 00190-9-72758

https://www.sanshusha.co.jp

編集担当 三井るり子

印刷所――倉敷印刷株式会社

―――――――――――――――――――――――――

©2020 Printed in Japan ISBN978-4-384-33497-5 C1082

表紙デザイン――――――山内宏一郎（SAIWAI DESIGN）

表紙イラスト――――――Giraffarte / PIXTA（ピクスタ）

本文デザイン――――――岩井栄子

準拠 CD 録音・制作――高速録音株式会社

【データ】問題作成時に BNC（小学館コーパスネットワーク）のデータを利用しています。

教科書準拠 CD 発売

本書の準拠 CD をご希望の方は弊社までお問い合わせください。